DIET FOR DREAMERS

INSPIRATION TO FEED YOUR DREAMS,
ENCOURAGEMENT TO FOSTER YOUR CREATIVITY!

DIET FOR DREAMERS

INSPIRATION TO FEED YOUR DREAMS,
ENCOURAGEMENT TO FOSTER YOUR CREATIVITY!

TOM ENGLISH AND
WILMA ESPAILLAT ENGLISH

RAVENS'
READS
AN IMPRINT OF DEAD LETTER PRESS
BOX 134, NEW KENT, VA 23124-0134

Diet for Dreamers
First published 2015 by Ravens' Reads
An imprint of
DEAD LETTER PRESS

This edition © 2015

Printed in the United States of America

ISBN-10: 0-9796335-7-5
ISBN-13: 978-0-9796335-7-7

FIRST EDITION
August 2015

DEAD LETTER PRESS
BOX 134, NEW KENT, VIRGINIA 23124-0134

CONTENTS:

Dieting for Dreamers

You are never too old to set another goal
or to dream a new dream.
—C. S. Lewis

If you can dream it, you can do it.
—Walt Disney

WE LAUNCHED A SERIES of internet articles called *Diet for Dreamers* on Martin Luther King, Jr. Day, January 19, 2015. This was a wholly fitting time to debut a weekly series created to encourage people in every walk of life who dare to dream big—and to feed their dreams.

Dr. King had a great dream that one day all people would live together in harmony—*equal,* and with equal rights; that all people would "one day live in a nation where they will not be judged by the color of their skin but by the content of their character." Have we arrived yet? Not really. We've made great strides along the course set by Dr. King, but when it comes to racial harmony there's still a great deal of tension, mistrust, and even civil unrest. But as we honor the man who showed us the way, we can do nothing greater, nothing nobler, than also to honor the dream of this great visionary; we must stay true to the course Dr. King set

1

before us, a narrow path of peaceful coexistence and honest communication, of understanding and trust.

Like Dr. King, we all have hopes and dreams: visions, goals, things we want to accomplish. For many of us, the dream looms before us like an imposing mountain peak, its summit shrouded in a mist of past failures and self-doubt. We often think we will never get there. We get overwhelmed, perhaps even paralyzed by fear and doubt. Sometimes we just give up. We allow the dream inside us to die. Why?

Most dreams, the really big ones, the ones worth fighting to keep alive, are too big to accomplish by ourselves, in our own strength and through our own efforts. Relying solely on our own abilities may never get us to where we want to be. To get to the top we need hope, perseverance, and faith in something greater than ourselves. For believers, it's important to remember these truths: *"I can do ALL things through Christ, who strengthens me."* (Philippians 4:13 NKJV)

Because: *"...with God ALL things are possible!"*

(Matthew 19:26 NKJV)

Say it! Believe it! Act on it! And dream again!

The internet series *Diet for Dreamers* appears each Monday on our website AngelAtTheDoor.com, along with our other series *Encouragement for Creators* (every Friday) and *Angel in the Kitchen* (Tuesdays and Thursdays). Five dozen of the best articles from *Diet for Dreamers* and its companion series *Encouragement for Creators* are collected here for your enjoyment.

Whether you're an artist or a writer, an actor or a singer; an inventor or an entrepreneur; or simply someone who dreams of better days ahead, we want to help you achieve your goals, by encouraging you to faithfully pursue your dreams while providing you with practical advice and inspiring stories. In this collection you'll discover fascinating facts and a few humorous turns about men and women, young and old, who dreamed big and succeeded despite shaky circumstances, overwhelming obstacles and, often, the silly notions of our wonderful, whacky world.

Tom English
Wilma Espaillat English
New Kent, VA

ABOUT THE AUTHORS:
Wilma Espaillat English *grew up in a bilingual, bicultural family in New York and New Jersey, learning firsthand the significance of hospitality in the Hispanic culture. Today she is a published writer, speaker and educator. She has taught a variety of subjects including Business English, Public Speaking, Spanish, and Ancient World History, at both the college and high school levels. She has written high school curriculum for classes in Multicultural Studies, and conducted seminars for civic groups, including law enforcement agencies. She also has taught Bible and Christian Life topics to adults ranging in age from 18 to 80. She is the wife of Tom English.*

Tom English *grew up in a "Southern fried" family in rural Virginia. Today he is a Senior Chemist at Newport News Shipbuilding. He is also a published writer and an award-nominated editor of both fiction and non-fiction. Most recently, his work has appeared in the print anthologies* Challenger Unbound *(KnightWatch Press) and* Gaslight Arcanum: Uncanny tales of Sherlock Holmes *(Edge SF & Fantasy). Tom also edited the mammoth* Bound for Evil: Curious Tales of Books Gone Bad, *a 2008 Shirley Jackson Award finalist for best anthology. Like his wife, Wilma, he has extensive knowledge in Biblical Studies and has taught many Christian Life classes to singles and "young" married couples ages 18 to 80. He resides with Wilma, surrounded*

3

by books and beasts, deep in the woods of New Kent, Virginia.

Tom and Wilma invite you to join them each weekday for humorous and inspiring new articles at their internet home, www.AngelAtTheDoor.com

Also available from Ravens' Reads:
ANGEL IN THE KITCHEN: TRUTH & WISDOM INSPIRED BY FOOD, COOKING, KITCHEN TOOLS AND APPLIANCES

Coming in April 2016:
DIET FOR DREAMERS: A SECOND SERVING!

Ravens' Reads: "Books to Feed Your Spirit!"

DIET FOR DREAMERS: DREAM AGAIN!

It's faith in something and enthusiasm for something that makes a life worth living.
> —Oliver Wendall Holmes, Sr.,
> (Physician, author and lecturer, 1809-1894)

Ever had a school teacher scold you for having your "head in the clouds"? Sure, daydreaming while you should be paying attention is counterproductive, but on the other hand, we all need dreams to be healthy and happy. Having a dream, a goal to accomplish, a project to complete, adds to our sense of purpose and self-worth—which in turn helps to give us hope. And we NEED hope! Without hope we lose spirit and eventually stop truly living. We lose our **enthusiasm** for life, and we find ourselves just going through the motions of everyday existence, shuffling along mindlessly like one of those zombies in *Night of the Living Dead*: no heart, no soul.

Forget milk. Got enthusiasm? Dr. Norman Vincent Peale, founder of the inspirational magazine *Guideposts*, wrote several volumes on the subject, but he managed to sum up the main idea in a single book title: *Enthusiasm Makes the Difference!*

Dr. Peale once wrote, "There is real magic in enthusiasm. It spells the difference between mediocrity and accomplishment."

Interestingly, the word enthusiasm means "full of God," which shouldn't be too surprising because, after all, it's God who created each of us and then filled us with life. So take heart when things go wrong, because God loves you, and He cares about you!

"Yes," you may think, "but does God care about my hopes and dreams?" Indeed He does! Read these words aloud:

"'For I know the plans I have for you,' declares the Lord, 'plans to prosper you, and not to harm you, plans to give you a hope and a future.'" (Jeremiah 29:11 NIV)

So trust God, and dream again!

"How do you go from where you are to where you wanna be? ...I think you have to have an enthusiasm for life. You have to have a dream, a goal. And you have to be willing to work for it."

—Jim Valvano
(NCSU Basketball coach and broadcaster, 1946-1993)

"Nothing great was ever achieved without enthusiasm."

—Ralph Waldo Emerson
(American poet and lecturer, 1803-1882)

No Fear!

One of the biggest hindrances to success is the fear of failure. While certain natural fears are healthy and beneficial—the ones that keep us out of trouble by warning us NOT to do something really stupid—this particular fear can be paralyzing. It can keep us from taking the next big step in the pursuit of our goals. It prompts us NOT to take chances, and instead, to make excuses, to be complacent, and to accept defeat before we even try!

In his daily devotional, The Word for You Today (2/25/15), evangelist Bob Gass states that researchers conducted an experiment in which "frogs were placed in separate glass jars covered with lids to prevent them from escaping. At first the frogs kept jumping, trying to escape, but each time they'd hit their heads on the lid. After thirty days of doing this, something amazing happened. When the lids were removed...the frogs never jumped out even though they could easily have done so. Why? Because they had formed a belief system that the top of the jar was as high as they could go...."

That describes a lot of us. At some level, we tried to go higher but we failed. And now we've stopped trying. We've stalled in the pursuit of goals, believing we can't go any further. We're reluctant to even try, because the taste of defeat is bitter, indeed, and we don't want to experience it again. So we tell ourselves, "I'm satisfied where I am. I've climbed high enough. I don't need to rise any higher. Maybe I don't deserve any better than this. Besides, I wouldn't succeed anyway."

If we allow this fear to rule our lives, we grow stagnant in every area. Playing it safe becomes our guiding principle in life. We'll only do the right thing as long as it's SAFE to do so. We'll stop investing our money, our time, our talents, our love—because there's a risk to every endeavor. There's always a chance we can be hurt or suffer a loss.

No risks, no deep relationships, no chances on anything except the tried and true. Is this playing it safe? Or is it bondage? Are we free to take chances, or slaves to our fear?

Jesus Christ repeatedly admonishes us "to not be afraid." In the Gospels alone there are dozens of warnings concerning FEAR. Our Lord came to free us— especially from bondage to fear: fear of not being worthy; fear of being rejected; fear of saying "No!" to unreasonable requests; fear of not living up to expectations; fear of failure; fear of being too young or too old or not qualified or over-qualified or too late or too early or not the right gender or ethnicity. To quote U.S. President Harry Truman, "We have nothing to fear but fear itself." And we needn't fear that one, either, because "There is no fear in love, but perfect love casts out fear." (John 4:18 ESV) God's love is perfect. So be FREE! Take confidence, strength and joy from the love, acceptance, and grace of God.

"For God has not given us a spirit of fear and timidity, but of power, love, and self-discipline."

(2 Timothy 1:7 NLT)

WITTY INVENTIONS!

Ever wonder at all the cool stuff that's been invented totally by accident? When a great idea suddenly falls in your lap, grab it! It's a gift from heaven. Stuff happens, and sometimes you just need to go with the flow. That's what Fred Morrison did. One day in 1938, he and his future wife Lucille were having fun on a beach in Santa Monica, California, tossing a cake pan back and forth. Apparently they appeared to be having so much fun— and the cake pan was spinning through the air so smoothly—that someone offered to purchase Fred's "flying disc" for 25 cents. The inventor, who'd always been fascinated with aerodynamics, later stated, "That got the wheels turning, because you could buy a cake pan for five cents, and if people on the beach were willing to pay a quarter for it, well...there was a business!"

It would have been easy to laugh off the whole incident, chalking it up as one of the many whimsies of our whacky world. Instead, the couple embraced the weird, and started selling 5-cent cake pans on the beach, at a quarter each! They continued their side business, collecting quite a few quarters, until the U.S. entered World War II. Fred Morrison signed up with the Army Air Force, and flew a P-47 Thunderbolt fighter plane until he was shot down and taken a prisoner of war. He spent 90 days as a POW, possibly thinking about how to improve the aerodynamic design of his cake pan.

After the war, He designed an improved flying disc, made of plastic, which he called the Whirlo-Way. In 1948, Morrison and a business partner began producing the discs, but following a wave of UFO sightings, they decided to market the toy as the "Flyin-Saucer."

The two men demonstrated the flying disc at fairs across the country, selling thousands at a buck apiece, to people who were amazed at the toy's ability to "hover." Morrison eventually went solo again, and in 1955 he designed a new model, the Pluto Platter, which was essentially the archetype of what we call a *Frisbee*. Morrison patented his design and sold the rights to the Wham-O Company in 1957. It was Wham-O co-founder Richard Knerr who decided to give the toy the official brand name Frisbee. The name was inspired by the Frisbie Pie Company of Bridgeport, Connecticut, and harkens back to the flying disc's origins as nothing more than a cake plate. Morrison hated the name, but in 1982, after receiving over $2 million in royalties, He told Forbes magazine, "I wouldn't change the name of it for the world."

So when a crazy idea comes sailing your way, seemingly out of nowhere, be bold and latch onto it. It might be nothing. Then again, it could be what you've been hoping for!

"I, wisdom, dwell with prudence, and find out knowledge of witty inventions." (Psalm 8:12 KJV)

TAKE AIM!

*Protect your enthusiasm from the negativity and fear
of others. Never decide to do nothing because you can
only do a little. Do what you can. You would be
surprised at what "little" acts have done for our world.*
—Steve Maraboli, *Unapologetically You:
Reflections on Life and the Human Experience*

We've all heard it: "If you fail to plan, you plan to fail."
Say *what?!* Nobody in his right mind plans to fail. Not
intentionally, anyway. But many of us do fail to plan.
We fail to set goals, map out what we want to
accomplish in life, and strategize how we'll go about
doing it.

If you don't shoot for something in life, then you're
not living life to its fullest. Or to put it another way, if
you don't aim for something, then you'll be...*well,
aimless!* Just shuffling along with no purpose and no
hope. Soon you'll start to shrivel spiritually.

The writer of Proverbs 29:18 teaches us that
"Where there is no vision, the people perish"; so don't
keep living aimlessly. Take aim!

Now, are you ready to fire away? Once you do take
aim, everything else boils down to strategy, your plan of
attack. Think of a war. Great wars are won with smaller
victories won in battles. Your goals will be achieved in

much the same way, through the small victories and accomplishments that move you closer to winning your bigger dreams.

And indeed, achieving a truly big dream is much like waging a war, to overcome the obstacles imposed by time, resources, circumstances, and even people who don't want to see you succeed (for various reasons). Are you strategizing to win the small battles you encounter each day?

Every morning you should map out your day. Make a list of things you need to do and want to accomplish. Prioritize your "to do list." Work to achieve something worthwhile every day. Little steps carefully planned each day can take you far along the path to success.

Novels are written a chapter at a time, chapters a few paragraphs at a time. And even four or five sentences a day can soon lead to an entire book. The key is: have a plan or a list or a strategy EVERY day to accomplish SOMETHING. Take aim in life for the long haul, but also take aim daily. Doing so will remind you of what most needs your attention, help you to stay focused and use your time wisely; and keep you moving forward and on the right track.

CRITICAL CARE FOR CREATORS

As long as some*one* some*where* is trying to accomplish some*thing*, there will be critics. And as long as there are critics in this world, you'll hear or read negative, even ugly, comments on just about everything under the sun. If you're a creator, inventor, entrepreneur, athlete, leader, business professional, or _____ (fill in the blank), your work and quite possibly you yourself, will be criticized at some point. Critics will take special aim at you—whether you deserve it or not. And a few will try to get in some cheap shots. Fact of life. So you need to learn to be bulletproof.

U.S. President Ronald Reagan, like many leaders before him, came under frequent attack while in office. We can imagine the political criticism of his policies, whether legitimate or unfounded—along with all the slurs, jokes, and trivialities that accompanied it—had to get old fast. But Reagan never seemed to get frazzled by his critics. In fact, the media labeled him The Teflon President, because nothing nasty that anybody was spouting seemed to stick. Reagan simply let everything slide off his back.

There are two kinds of criticism: valid and invalid. If you encounter valid criticism (Truth), try to learn from it and improve. "To one who listens, valid criticism is like a gold earring...." (Proverbs 25:12 NLT) However, if you encounter invalid criticism (unwarranted, untrue, or immaterial), take it with a grain of salt. Never allow such barbs to pull you down. Think about the motivations behind invalid criticism:

1. Money: There are professional critics who get paid to "evaluate" books, movies, music, sporting events, food, restaurants, public figures—you name it. The best of these critics try to be honest, unbiased and realistic. The worst are nitpickers who find great pleasure in exposing the minutest flaws and tearing things apart, usually to be entertaining. Face it, critics get paid to be critical. Many feel if they can't find something wrong, they're not doing their job thoroughly. Weigh the value of their OPINIONS, and discard any unjust or unfounded criticism. Then move forward.

2. Jealousy: We need to explain this one? Seriously? Okay, there will always be people who are envious of your accomplishments, especially if THEY aren't successful. Writing or saying bad things is often an attempt to minimize what you've achieved, and justify their own shortcomings. Some people try to lift themselves up by lowering others. Soar above it!

3. Fear: No one wants to be left behind! Your friends and family may fear you'll succeed, while they won't. By the way, fear and jealousy are critical collaborators. Negative comments from a fearful person should elicit a degree of compassion. Smile and encourage these cowering critics. Don't take their words to heart.

4. Competitiveness: You may not know this—*heh!*—but people are competitive. We're born that way: a baby will compete for a mother's attention; children quickly learn games rooted in competition; teenagers compete for friends and acceptance; students for scholastic honors and college placements; and adults in the workplace jockey for career advancements. It's best to not allow this motivator to rule your life and control your thoughts and actions. Many do, though. So, when they try to minimize your achievements, don't allow their negative comments to DISTRACT you from your personal goals.

5. Pessimism and negativity: Some people are just plain negative. Some actually have a critical spirit; and these people will always find something to complain about, something to nitpick. Antidote: continue to be positive; let these people pick their nits. You have more important concerns.

There will always be critics in your life, people who don't want to see you rise higher; who may even hope you fail; people who want you to stay right where you are! Understand the motivations behind invalid criticism. Love the critic, but let the criticism bounce off you. How did Jesus respond to His critics? For the most part, He didn't. He stayed focused on His mission and mostly ignored them. Go, and do thou likewise!

"We serve God whether people honor us or despise us, whether they slander us or praise us." (2 Corinthians 6:8 NLT)

GOT REJECTION?

No prophet is accepted in his hometown.
—Luke 4:24 NIV

Who said that? Jesus Christ, right after he got rejected in, of all places, the village where He grew up—and Jesus was the greatest teacher and the best storyteller who ever walked this planet, bar none! Remember all those cool parables, the ones we're still reading and referencing today—almost 2000 years after He shared them? Of course. How many modern writers continue to riff on "The Story of The Good Samaritan" or "The Prodigal Son"? How many financial experts on "The Parable of the Talents"? And yet, even Jesus faced his share of rejection in that arena. In fact, rejection, for Jesus, was always in the plan. He had to be rejected before he could be exalted, put down before He was lifted up. And if people rejected Jesus (!!!)...well, we ought to be able to handle a little rejection ourselves. Consider it a rite of passage. You won't be anyone special until you've received your share of rejection.

Know who else got rejected? Do you have a favorite author? Yes, him too. Yeah, her also. Obviously your favorite writers didn't give up. They stayed the course no matter how hard it got or how long it took. You need to do the same.

Want to hear something funny? Dr. Laurence J. Peter submitted a non-fiction manuscript to McGraw-Hill in 1964. An astute editor at the publishing company responded: "I can foresee no commercial possibilities for such a book and consequently can offer no encouragement." Undeterred, Dr. Peter sent the manuscript to thirty other publishers and received thirty more rejections. Finally, William Morrow & Co. purchased his book for a single payment of $2,500; and the publisher's expectations for it were so low that the company ordered an extremely cautious print run of only 10,000 copies. But hey, editors and publishers are only human: how could they know—despite being in the business of recognizing profitable book projects—that *The Peter Principle* would rocket to the top of the *New York Times* best-sellers list?; or that the book would sell 200,000 copies its first year in print?; or be translated into 38 languages? Good grief, it's a good thing the good doctor didn't give up on a good book idea! (How's that for a good sentence?)

Got Rejection? Welcome to an elite club that boasts a membership comprised of the world's best and greatest. Next, we'll share Jesus' advice to those who receive a rejection slip

SHAKE IT OFF!

If you've had your work rejected, be it a manuscript, a song, a painting, or what have you, then you're part of a special club comprised of the who's who of great men and women. The membership list of this club staggers the imagination, because every artist, writer, musician—and absolutely anyone else who's ever tried to get somewhere in this life—has faced his or her share of rejection.

By the way, who's the most rejected person who ever walked the planet? During the course of this book we'll share the stories of some of the runners-up, dreamers who repeatedly had doors slammed in their faces, but who refused to throw in the towel; and who, because of their perseverance, eventually found great success. The prize, however, goes to Jesus Christ. He encountered enough rejection for a lifetime. No, actually more than that: count all the people who've ever lived and ever will live, because that's how many lifetimes worth of rejection He endured. And He endured it for us! So, who besides Christ would know the absolute best medicine for rejection?

Jesus admonished His disciples that wherever they carried their message, when they encountered rejection they were to "shake it off!" When you get a "NO!" or have a door slammed in your face, remember the Lord's advice: "If anyone will not welcome you or listen to your words, leave that home or town and shake the dust off your feet." (Matthew 10:14 NIV)

In other words, when you get knocked down just get up, brush yourself off, and keep on knocking and trying. Dust? It's a perfect analogy. The fallout from rejection, the hurt and disappointment, the fear and doubt, the desire to quit, all of it tends to settle upon us like dust. Get rejected enough times and you'll be so caked with it that you won't be able to see or feel or breathe. That's why Jesus warns us to shake it all off, and keep our feet moving! Never give up. Never lie down and let the dust of rejection cover you over until it's impossible for anyone to ever know you passed along this way.

Follow the example of motivational speaker and writer Jack Canfield. The first month he and Mark Victor Hansen tried to sell their manuscript for a new kind of book, they got the door slammed in their faces 33 times. New York publishers told them "anthologies don't sell" because "nobody wants to read a book of short little stories." Besides, stated one publisher, the book is "too nicey-nice"! And the long line of NO!s didn't end there. "You know," Canfield once said, "my first...book was rejected by 140 publishers, over the course of 18 months. If we had given up at the first rejection or the 100th rejection, I wouldn't be here before you." (From an interview posted Apr. 12, 2012 at ibnlive.in.com)

Finally, in 1993, Health Communications, a small, struggling publisher on the verge of bankruptcy, took a chance on the collection of poems, stories, and nuggets of encouragement. The gamble didn't just pay off, it saved the publishing company; because today, the 65-title *Chicken Soup for the Soul* series has sold over 125 million copies in more than three dozen languages!

Got rejection? Shake it off! Get back on your feet. Keep walking. Keep trying. Keep moving forward, because success could be just around the next corner.

REJECTION GIANT!

If you've faced rejection as a creator, then you're part of a special club with a membership list that staggers the imagination, because every successful artist, writer, musician—and absolutely anyone else who's ever tried to get somewhere in this life—has faced his or her share of rejection.

Here's the story of how one man with a big vision overcame rejection and some incredible obstacles to create something that's been enjoyed by millions.

David Puttnam had been a producer in the film industry for not quite a decade, working mostly on documentaries or smaller movie productions. Sometime around 1980 he came across a true story that captured his imagination. The British producer thought it would make a good movie, but it would be one of those quiet little films: about the human spirit, about dreams, about overcoming prejudice and physical adversity. Puttnam felt he could produce his little movie for under $6 million, and he started looking for a studio to back the film. Here he encountered the first of many obstacles he would need to overcome to get the project off the ground: All the major UK studios turned the project down! Puttnam says he reached a point where he was "thinking of pulling the plug. That, or remortgage the house." Then, in 1981, the Egyptian shipping magnate Al Fayed agreed to put up half the money. Fayed joked to Putnam, "You've been fairly around the track before you get to Egyptian shipping lines."

Puttnam was on his way, or so he thought. All he needed now was an American studio to bankroll the rest of the film project. So the producer went out and hired Hugh Hudson to direct his movie. Hudson had never before directed a feature film, but he had been an ad man and had done a few documentaries; and he was excited about the new opportunity. Sound promising? Hang on. Hudson started his new job by casting a handful of virtually unknown actors for all the lead roles.

Meanwhile, Puttnam had been combing the U.S. for weeks, searching for a studio to back the rest of the film. Another stretch of hard road: "The American studios rejected it," Hudson once stated. "Because the two main characters barely meet. There is no shoot-out at the end." Puttnam added, "I remember sitting...in a hotel room almost weeping. It seemed impossible to get anybody to understand why this was a film worth investing in." Finally, Twentieth-Century Fox stepped in with the rest of the money.

First-time feature film director Hudson then shot the movie in 10 weeks, and he managed to do it for only $5.5 million. Happy ending? Not yet. The producer Puttnam now faced an uphill slog to find a studio willing to distribute the movie. He remembers how the production head of one U.S. studio slipped out of a screening to go to the bathroom and never came back. "We never saw him again." But Puttnam didn't give up.

He did, however, finally reach a point of desperation. Seemingly out of options, Puttnam offered the film as a made-for-TV movie. Ironically, the head of a major network "turned it down flat. He didn't want to buy it at any price." But sometimes a closed door is a good thing: "We were saved from going to TV because they didn't think it was good enough." That's when Warner Bros. offered to distribute the film theatrically.

Putnam's little movie, directed by a newbie, starring a cast of unknowns, featuring the story of two men who were all but forgotten, opened at a single venue in New York, the 700-seat Guild theater. Its first week, the film made $70,000. Compared to the box office receipts of today's big-budget movies, this may not sound like much, but remember, this was the take from a single theater! Soon critics were praising Puttnam's tale of the 1924 Olympic Games, word of mouth from satisfied audiences spread like wildfire, and the movie went on to gross over $75 million worldwide. But the coolest thing, from an artist's standpoint, is that *Chariots of Fire* was awarded 4 Oscars, including the Best Picture of the Year!

So ask yourself, do you feel like an artistic "David" facing a Goliath of rejection? Pick up your creative slingshot and take aim, dear friends.

THE GREAT MYSTERY OF REJECTION

For most of us, the *how's* and *why's* of rejection remain a mystery. It's not always about talent, or the lack of it. Timing and taste are assuredly factors. Fate and fickleness also seem to play a part.

In 1882, a bored, young doctor began to dabble in writing. His earliest pieces were, by his own admission, largely embarrassing efforts; but he stuck with his new hobby and, a few years later, completed his first novel, which he promptly and proudly sent out to a publisher. Unfortunately, he lived during an extremely barbaric period of history when there were no photocopiers, and his only copy of the manuscript was lost in the mail!

Undeterred, the good doctor continued to scribble his thoughts, and soon completed his second novel, which he promptly and proudly mailed off. No, this time he took the precaution of keeping a copy. Actually, he made several copies, so he was able to send the novel to several different publishers. A few weeks later he received by return post, several different rejections—enough, in fact, to convince him to shelve the book.

Finally, in 1886, he finished a third novel. The first three publishers he approached rejected it immediately, one of them stating that the tale is "Neither long enough for a serial nor short enough for a single story." The fourth publisher agreed to print the tale, in one of the many popular magazines of the time, and paid him the meager sum of £25—less than most magazines paid for a single short story. But at least his third novel did see print. For one whole month it was on the newsstands, but the next month it was gone and forgotten.

So the young doctor didn't immediately quit his day job. He continued seeing his patients and continued to dream of writing full time. Ironically, he didn't consider the publication of this first novel a turning point in his career. He was thoroughly pleased with the novel, and he genuinely cared for its two main characters, but he knew that as writer, he had a long way to go. His turning point, or so he thought at the time, came when he was asked to write the English translation of a German article entitled "Testing Gas Pipes for Leakage."

Not very glamorous, but the editor had approached him, and commissioned him to do the piece. Was he on his way to being a real writer at last? Did he have a bright future penning articles about leaky pipes? Yes and no, respectively.

In 1989, *Lippincott's Monthly Magazine* asked Sir Arthur Conan Doyle to write a second novel featuring the now immortal characters of Sherlock Holmes and his trusted associate Dr. John H. Watson, M.D. Conan Doyle penned *The Sign of Four* as a follow-up to his first published novel, *A Study in Scarlet*, the one for which he was so handsomely paid £25. The rest of the story is literary history: four novels, 56 short stories, as well as any number of unauthorized adventures called pastiches; movies and TV shows, dating from the era of silent films all the way up to the current BBC hit *Sherlock* and ABC's *Elementary*.

So there you have it: one of the most successful and well-known literary characters rose up like a phoenix from the ashes of Conan Doyle's rejected novel. We're all grateful that somebody was willing to publish the first adventure of the World's Greatest Consulting Detective. It's yet another case that proves the point: the mystery of rejection is strange indeed!

Imagination, Ingenuity, & Initiative Pay Off!

Sometimes having a big budget really pays off. Other times....

RKO Pictures once enjoyed status as one the major Hollywood studios. A few of us may remember the studio chiefly for the legendary 1933 film *King Kong*, a special effects extravaganza that astounded moviegoers in its day. RKO also was famous for its madcap romantic comedies, and had produced a string of popular and profitable movies starring Ginger Rogers and Fred Astaire. At some point, however, the studio went into a financial nosedive: a handful of artistic giants had made their way into the control tower at RKO.

Bigger became a production byword at RKO, and in 1941, after giving free reign to director Orson Welles, the studio released its biggest picture yet, *Citizen Kane*; and although the movie was a critical success—today it's considered one of the greatest movies ever made—it lost mega-money at the box-office. (Quick, someone say "Rosebud!") A few months later RKO followed up with another commercial failure directed by Welles, *The Magnificent Ambersons*. Like *Citizen Kane*, the movie was critically acclaimed but came in way over budget. RKO quickly aborted Welles' third film, but the damage had already been done. RKO had lost close to $2 Million.

RKO needed to get out of debt, fast! But to do so they needed to make some profitable movies—on shoe-string budgets. Tarzan would help save the day. Johnny Weissmuller swung into the role and starred in six crowd-pleasing movies for RKO that made use of stock footage of African wildlife. George Sanders and his brother Tom Conway also did their parts, in numerous entries in the inexpensive but highly entertaining mystery franchises *The Saint* and *The Falcon*.

The real savior of RKO, however, was Val Lewton. This little-known filmmaker had worked on the classics *A Tale of Two Cities* and *Gone with the Wind*. When Lewton arrived at RKO he found he had his work cut out for him. At a time when the other major studios were producing movies with budgets of over $500,000 each, RKO asked Lewton to make them a movie for less than $150,000. On top of that, RKO wanted a horror picture, because Universal Studios was having so much success with their slew of Frankenstein and Mummy movies. Then, just to add insult to injury they saddled Lewton with a title for the picture: "Cat People"!

Lewton probably shook his head in disbelief and asked "Seriously?" But instead of walking he started working: he assembled a team of writers and directors that included Robert Wise, who'd go on to later fame and fortune directing *The Sound of Music* and *West Side Story*.

In 1942, the horror picture *Cat People*, directed by first-timer Jacques Tourneur, premiered. Val Lewton had produced the movie with the improbable title, but had worked from an original screenplay based on his own 1930 short story "The Bagheeta." The film was moody and atmospheric, but there were no monsters and nothing at all grisly took place in front of the camera. Lewton had seen an opportunity and had taken the initiative; but instead of making a run-of-the-mill horror movie, he had created a psychological study that relied more on imagination than special effects, and on ingenuity to overcome obstacles.

RKO probably looked at the movie and wondered what had they gotten themselves into now. But *Cat People*, costing a mere $141,659, brought in almost $4 million in its first two years. And Val Lewton? He had saved the studio from financial disaster. RKO quickly rewarded their savior, by asking Lewton to continue to make really inexpensive horror movies with really stupid titles. And definitely the worst title RKO stuck Lewton with: *I Walked with a Zombie!*

Lewton didn't let it ruin his day. He made another incredibly intelligent and memorable film. And before he left the studio, Lewton had made eight of the coolest, most highly re-garded movies in RKO's history.

Imagination will always trump budget; and initiative and ingenuity will win the day. So no matter what you're facing, keep your chin up. And seize your opportunities. Above all, "Do not despise these small beginnings, for the LORD rejoices to see the work begin...." (Zechariah 4:10 NLT)

THE CHOCOLATIER
WHO PERSEVERED

Nothing says LOVE quite like chocolate. At least, that's how the man who created Milk Chocolate Kisses felt. In fact, Milton S. Hershey was actually saddened that the rich, dark confection was available only to the wealthy, and even then, often only for special occasions. Hershey had big dreams of making chocolate both available and affordable to the general public. He dreamed of a day when the treat would be commonplace, and every day, everyone could have a chocolate kiss. But some of his sweet dreams could have ended up being lost at sea!

Hershey was born September 13, 1857. A descendant of Swiss and German ancestors, young Hershey grew up in a Pennsylvania Mennonite community. The future American entrepreneur originally spoke only Pennsylvania Dutch language, but that wouldn't deter him from success in a mostly English-speaking business world. Hershey's father was something of a rover, and often left his wife and son for extended periods. As a result, Milton Hershey was forced to quit school after the 4th grade. But that wasn't to be a deterrent to fame, fortune and philanthropy, either.

Backed financially by his mother's family, Milton Hershey moved to Philadelphia in 1876 and started his first candy business. After only six years, the business went bankrupt, in 1882. Still undeterred, Milton started a second confectionery business a year later, this time in New York. Although initially successful, his new venture went belly up after three years.

Hershey returned to Lancaster, PA in 1886. His dream of bringing confections to the masses was still undimmed. So, using a candy recipe he'd picked up somewhere along the bumpy road to success, Hershey started the Lancaster Caramel Company. This business took off, producing sizable financial rewards and firmly establishing Hersey as a candy maker.

Hershey hadn't made history yet, but he was about to. Hershey was enthusiastic about the potential of milk chocolate—at the time a luxury product available only to the upper class. He was determined to find a way to economically produce and sell it to the general public. So he sold his caramel company in 1900 and purchased a large piece of dairy land about 30 miles northwest of Lancaster, a move which ensured him large supplies of fresh milk for his cooking experiments.

Success: how sweet it is! Hershey overcame obstacles and persevered; and a few months later, he introduced the Hershey Milk Chocolate Bar. It's very tempting to stop typing here, so we can run out to the kitchen and grab one—preferably with almonds. Yes, right now! Because we love chocolate! Actually, we're chocoholics! (Don't judge us!) But we need to keep typing long enough to let you know Hershey's tale isn't over yet. Far from it. The man went on to make many more valuable contributions to the lives of Americans. He had new dreams to fulfill. But for a quirk of fate, these fabulous new visions might never have been realized. Everything—including the beloved "candy man" himself, might have been lost at sea. Join us for the tasty conclusion to this rich story!

Sweet, Satisfying, & Inspiring

In the late 1800s, the American candy maker Milton S. Hershey had a dream to make chocolate both available and affordable to the general public. Despite two failed business ventures, Hershey persevered and, in 1900, he introduced the first Hersey Milk Chocolate Bar. (Read the "The Chocolatier Who Persevered.") But the candy man's dreams and creations went further. Seven years later, he developed and treated Americans to Hershey's Kisses! The following year he gave us the Hershey Bar with Almonds!

But Hershey's innovations and contributions went far beyond chocolate. In his future were more creations, as well as numerous acts of philanthropy. Hershey truly wanted to help people in any way he could. Fortunately for all of us, he got his chance. But things might have turned out differently were it not for a sudden business matter Hershey needed to address on April 10, 1912. Before we explain further, we'll con-tinue with Milton Hershey's accomplishments and acts of kindness.

In 1905, he completed construction on the world's largest chocolate manufacturing company—eat your heart out, Willy Wonka!—in the center of a dairy farm-ing district in Pennsylvania. Soon after, his delicious milk chocolate became the first nationally-marketed brand of candy.

But Hershey didn't stop there: with his support, homes, shops, churches, and a transportation system sprang up around his chocolate factory. In 1909, he established the Hershey Industrial School to help disadvantaged kids. He also founded a teaching hospital with an initial endowment of $50 million. Hershey once stated, "One is only happy in proportion as he makes others feel happy and only useful as he contributes his influences for the finer callings in life."

Hershey's company continued to spread happiness. During WWII his chocolate factory supplied the U.S. Armed Forces with specially made chocolate bars. No small feat. The bars—two types, the Ration "D" Bar and the Tropical Chocolate Bar—had to meet stringent military requirements. They had to weigh one or two ounces each, and resist melting at temperatures higher than 90 degrees. No problem!

Between 1940 and 1945, the Hershey plant produced and distributed over 3 billion chocolate bars to soldiers throughout the world. At the height of production the company was making 24 million chocolate ration bars a week, and it ultimately received five Army-Navy "E" Production Awards for exceeding expectations for quality and quantity. (Sorry, Charley!) And, of course, the famous Hershey Park and Hershey Museum were yet to come. Milton Hershey's many contributions are remembered there, and kids young and old delight to tour the chocolate factory.

Thank God this great man, who gave us so much, needed to attend to some last minute business affairs on the morning of April 10, 1912. You see, Hershey and his wife had booked passage from Southampton, England to New York on the maiden voyage of the ill-fated British luxury liner RMS Titanic. But something concerning the chocolate company suddenly came up, forcing the couple to cancel their reservations at the last minute! *Whew!!*

Hershey lived happily to the ripe old age of 88, blessing millions of people with his kindness and candy.

"The steps of a good man are ordered by the Lord...." (Psalm 37:23 King James)

TAKE YOUR VITAMINS!

If we're going to be healthy, we need lots of Vitamin D in our diets. If we're going to achieve our dreams, or be successful at anything, we also need another kind of "Vitamin D"!

There are three major types of Vitamin D that are vital to good health. Fortunately, someone decided to make things easy on us by simply calling these vitamins, D1 to D3. We get these from foods and sunlight, but nutritionists recommend taking Vitamin D supplements. Interestingly, doctors rarely, if ever, see or hear about someone who's had too much Vitamin D in their diet. On the other hand, being deficient in "D" can cause major problems.

You'll be amazed at how similar the *Dreamer's D* supplement is to the nutritional supplement. There are three types of Dreamer's D, it's vital for success, and you can't have too much of it. Before we explain exactly what Dreamer's D is, let's list the health benefits of regular Vitamin D. As you read them, think about how each benefit can also apply to achieving your goals.

Vitamin D strengthens our bones, allowing us to stand—and to stand strong! It increases our immunity, helping us to resist attacks. It protects our minds, enabling us to stay focused. It strengthens our hearts, allowing us to live longer and better lives. It even combats depression!

There are three types of Dreamer's D:

D1 is Decision: decide what you want out of life; decide what you want to accomplish in life; decide how you'll achieve these things. Then make a decision to get started. You'll never lose weight, look for a better job, sever a wrong relationship, put a stop to a destructive habit, or achieve any goal until you first purpose in your heart to do so. Doing the right thing starts with deciding what the right thing is! And you'll never follow through on anything until you DECIDE it's something YOU really want to do. Start deciding. Decisions are all about choices. Making them and sticking by them.

D2 is Discipline: you'll need this if you're serious about accomplishing anything in life. You can't hold down a job, maintain a relationship, stay out of trouble, stay out of debt, stay healthy, stay focused, or stay on track until you add lots of Discipline to your Dreamers' Diet. And just like the nutritional supplement, we need more of this "D"; never less. We all want to achieve our dreams. We all want something. But the unpleasant truth about life is that everything comes with a price, every achievement involves W.O.R.K! The work is always hard. Sometimes the work is no fun. But discipline is about getting the work done, even when your heart's not in it; even when you're tired; even when adversity strikes; even if people criticize you. Muhammad Ali always wanted to box. But staying in the training ring took discipline: "I hated every minute of training, but I said, 'Don't quit. Suffer now and live the rest of your life as a champion.'"

D3 works synergistically with D1 and D2. But it can be the hardest pill to swallow. There are tens of thousands of people who have D1 and D2 in their Dream Diets, but you'll never hear about these people. You'll never know their names. They're dreamers just like you. But sadly, they never go beyond the dream stage. They never took their D3.

D3 is DOING! After all, nothing ever gets started until someone makes a start. So take your vitamins and get going. DECIDE what you want to achieve, DISCIPLINE yourself to reach your goal, and then just DO IT!

THE PRICE OF FAME

He was an accomplished actor of both stage and film, a soft-spoken gentleman with refined features, a distinctive voice, and an air of gentility. He was a well-travelled connoisseur of fine wine and food, who enjoyed collecting interesting and unusual recipes from the places he visited, a hobby that led to his writing three cookbooks. He had a degree in art history, a subject about which he frequently lectured and wrote books.

He established himself as an actor in the 1944 film noir classic *Laura*, starring Gene Tierney; he gave voice to the radio show crime fighter Simon Templar in *The Saint*; he was a leading man in several Hollywood films, including *The House of the Seven Gables* and *Dragonwyck*; he portrayed such famous historical figures as Joseph Smith, Prince Albert, Richard III and Sir Walter Raleigh; he costarred with such A-list actors as Gregory Peck, Ronald Coleman, Ava Gardner, Tyrone Power, and Charles Laughton; he played priests and prosecutors, doctors and dandies. Imagine his shock, when Vincent Price suddenly found himself typecast as a villain, and trapped in horror movie roles!

Vincent Leonard Price, Jr. was born in Saint Louis, Missouri in 1911. He was the offspring of a prosperous and prominent family of entrepreneurs: his grandfather, Vincent Clarence, secured the family fortune, when he invented "Dr. Price's Baking Powder," the first cream of tartar baking powder; and his father, Vincent Leonard, Sr., was the president of the National Candy Company. Vincent Price graduated from Yale University, where he wrote for the campus humor magazine, *The Yale Record.* After teaching for a year, he entered the University of London, intending to work on his Master's degree, but was lured away by the call of the theatre.

Ultimately, Price appeared on stage, television, radio, and in over one hundred films. He enjoyed a career that lasted over fifty years, and spanned the genres of film noir, drama, mystery, thriller, comedy and horror. And he has two stars on the Hollywood Walk of Fame: one for motion pictures, one for television. He was an intelligent and refined performer, a multi-talented actor who ended up starring in an almost uninterrupted string of horror films and TV shows, starting with *House of Wax* in 1953, and lasting until about 1983.

How did Price feel about playing bloodthirsty madmen for over a quarter of a century? He took it all in stride, making the most of each and every role, enjoying himself and—dare we say it?—laughing all the way to bank!

Sometimes our talents take us places we never dreamed or expected. It may not be exactly what we planned, perhaps not even what we trained for, but we need to make the most of every opportunity—or setback. In other words, if life gives you lemons, make lemonade.

Flourish despite your circumstances—and bloom where you're planted. Price did this. He didn't simply resign himself to acting in horror movies; he took ownership of each role, brought all his talent to the table, elevated the genre to almost an art form, and went down in history as The Master of the Macabre. If we were going to be scared to death, we'd want Vincent

Price, suave and sophisticated, to do the scaring. And he did, in *House of Usher*, *The Pit and the Pendulum*, *The Tingler*, *The Bat* and many other movies.

"Live wisely...and make the most of every opportunity." (Colossians 4:5 NLT) "And we know that in all things God works for the good of those who love him, who have been called according to his purpose." (Romans 8:28 NIV)

LEIGH WHO?!?

This is the story of a tough cookie named Leigh. No, not Leigh Halfpenny, the rough and tumble rugby player from Wales; Leigh Brackett, one of the best American writers you've probably never heard of!

In a career spanning four decades, Brackett banged out over sixty short stories, more than a dozen novels—mostly science fiction and fantasy—as well as scripted several movies now considered to be Hollywood classics. Brackett had a knack for injecting mystery and noir elements into SF, and the writer also penned a few excellent crime novels. The film director Howard Hawks was so impressed with the first of these crime novels, *No Good from a Corpse*, that he told his secretary to call in "this guy Brackett" to help script the 1946 Humphrey Bogart movie *The Big Sleep*. That marked the beginning of Brackett's long association with Hollywood. The novelist went on to write television scripts for *Alfred*

Hitchcock Presents, and several more screenplays for Hawks, including four classic John Wayne movies: *Rio Bravo* (1959), *Hatari!* (1962), *El Dorado* (1966) and *Rio Lobo* (1970). Brackett excelled at writing tough guy cowpokes, big game hunters, and world-weary gumshoes; so when George Lucas decided his second Star Wars movie should focus more on rapscallion space-pirate Han Solo, he asked SF novelist Brackett to write the screenplay.

Sounds like Brackett could do no wrong, right? Well, not in the eyes of Bogart—at least not initially. Bogie definitely had to go through a period of adjustment once Brackett started co-writing with the great American novelist William Faulkner on Howard Hawks' detective movie *The Big Sleep.* The actor had played both hard-nosed gumshoes and ruthless gangsters, and he knew exactly how his character's dialogue should sound. But suddenly he was getting pages of a shooting script with lines that made his character, tough P.I. Phillip Marlowe, sound more like a prim school marm. He wasted no time confronting Brackett, the novice screenwriter, with his concerns.

But Bogie had to back up. The rotten lines he'd been given to read were not the work of Brackett; they'd been penned by Faulkner! Why did Bogie immediately assume Brackett was to blame? The answer had absolutely nothing to do with Brackett's inexperience as a screenwriter. No, Bogie figured all the *namby-pamby* lines just had to have come from Brackett's typewriter, because—oh, the indignity—Leigh Brackett was, to borrow a word from Philip Marlowe, a dame!

What? You thought Leigh was a guy? Because he— *er, SHE*—wrote scripts and novels about tough guys? Hey, we never said Leigh was a guy. But yeah, there *are* both men and women with the name *Leigh*, so we'll let you slide. Bogie, on the other hand, was guilty of a little literary male chauvinism! Turns out all the good lines he'd been getting, the snappy smart-guy patter that nailed Bogie's character, were the work of a 21 year-old female. To the actor's credit Bogart acknowledged his silly stereotyping, and then demanded that Brackett write ALL of his dialogue!

Regardless of gender, ethnicity, age, or experience, if you're a savvy creator, you can create whatever the job requires. So go for it! "My heart is stirred by a noble theme...my tongue is the pen of a skillful writer." (Psalm 45:1 NIV)

STOP & SMELL THE ROSES

A walk a day keeps the gloomies away!
—Norman Vincent Peale

What does the heart need to be healthy? Well, the heart of a dreamer needs a steady diet of joy and laughter, because nothing can kill creativity or zap our motivation and enthusiasm faster than a lack of joy.

What is joy? It's a sense of wellbeing; inner peace and optimism regardless of what's going on around you. We may not have control over bad situations, adverse circumstances or negative people, but we can have control over how we handle what life throws our way. We can walk around gloomy all day, our mouths puckered up from eating sour grapes, crying over spilled milk items; or we can choose to have joy!

That's right, joy is NOT a feeling, it's a choice.

Allow us to prescribe a "dietary supplement" to help restore your joy—similar to the remedy described by the great American writer Ray Bradbury in his short story "A Medicine for Melancholy"! Nothing we share will be hard to swallow, no bitter pills here, just a dose of delightful diversion. And fear not, you'll never OD on what we're dispensing.

Here's a big spoonful of Joy Juice, so open wide....

Symptoms: We dreamers can get so obsessed with achieving our goals, so focused on fulfilling our dreams that we lose sight of all the beauty in life. We trudge through the days with our eyes so fixed on the prize, so determined to reach our next destination on our chosen road to success, that we fail to enjoy the journey itself. Don't get us wrong, getting there is important, but it's possible to be too focused, too driven. Hey, there's miles of gorgeous scenery to the left and right of you if you'll just take a moment to admire it.

Cure: Set goals, be disciplined, stay focused, but don't overdo it. Stop once in a while to smell the roses! (We mean this both literally and figuratively!) Continue to pursue your dreams but make frequent stops to take in all the wonderful sights, sounds, and people you en-counter along the journey! Don't let life pass you by as one big blur!

Symptoms: When you find yourself getting irritable, snappy, easily angered and annoyed by every little thing—when you find yourself constantly in "fight mode" —then you're ready for some much needed R&R.

Cure: Get out and do something fun. Change your routine! Give your goals a rest and go shopping. Have an ice cream cone—with sprinkles! Curl up with a good magazine and even take a nap! Get outdoors and enjoy God's creation. Go for a walk in the park or on the beach. Find a nature trail. Take in a sunset (or a sunrise)!

When you find yourself getting down and mopey, it's time to refocus: think about how far you've come, not how far you've still to go; what you've accomplished, not what you've yet to achieve. Above all, start focusing on what you have, not what you want. Count your blessings: if you enjoy good health, have running hot water, a roof over your head, something good to eat, eyes and ears to take in all the beauty in life, and loved ones with whom you can share these things, then you are indeed wealthy.

BEING A BARNABAS

Sometimes talent and enthusiasm aren't enough. Sometimes what you know or what you can accomplish aren't as important as who you know. This is a sad but true fact of life. Just check your history books. Christopher Columbus had an incredible dream and the chutzpah to chase it all the way to "The New World"; but until he received the support and financial backing of King Ferdinand and Queen Isabella of Spain, Captain Columbus was going nowhere fast.

Have you ever felt like you were spinning your wheels on the road to success? Understand that to achieve certain goals, to fulfill some dreams, you may need a little help from someone with specialized skills, experience, connections, or capital. A "friend" who's willing to lend a helping hand, give some guidance, introduce you to the right people. You may need an agent, a mentor, a facilitator, a collaborator. You may need a Barnabas.

What's a Barnabas? A person who's willing to help another complete their "mission" in life. Someone who can open the right door for you, point you in the right direction, and get you started on your way. In the Book of Acts, there was a man named Barnabas who did this for the Apostle Paul, and the Gentile Church owes this facilitator a great debt of gratitude.

The Apostle Paul had a dream and a mission: to begin spreading the Good News of Jesus Christ to all the world—namely, the Gentiles. And Paul was the best person for the job. He had the knowledge, the experience and the wisdom—and the guidance of God's Holy Spirit. Paul had "the right stuff," but not the right connections. Actually, Paul had no connections, and no friends among the Jewish followers of Christ. What Paul did have was an extremely bad reputation. Seems that before believing in Christ, the Apostle Formerly Known as Saul had a track record of persecuting his Jewish brethren, and he'd been responsible for the deaths of many of them. Paul had changed, but in the eyes of Jewish believers, he was an unknown quantity, a liability, perhaps even a risk.

Despite his passion and his qualifications, Paul wasn't going anywhere as far as the Jewish leadership were concerned. "When Saul arrived in Jerusalem, he tried to meet with the believers, but they were all afraid of him. They did not believe he had truly become a believer!" (Acts 9:26 NLT) That's when Barnabas, the quintessential facilitator and all-around nice guy, stepped forward. "Then Barnabas brought him to the apostles and told them how Saul had seen the Lord on the way to Damascus and how the Lord had spoken to Saul. He also told them that Saul had preached boldly in the name of Jesus in Damascus." (Acts 9:26-27 NLT) Not only did Barnabas vouch for Paul, but he also joined the apostle on his mission. Barnabas helped Paul to achieve his objective and to fulfill his dream.

Sooner or later we all need a little help. Sooner or later we all need a Barnabas. We need for someone to put in a good word, help us with a project, or just be a good friend. No matter how self-sufficient we are, we can accomplish even more with a little help from our friends. Okay, so where do we find a Barnabas in a society filled with people who only look out for themselves? For that matter, why aren't there more Barnabas people in the world? Well, if we want the world to be filled with Barnabas people, we all need to start being Barnabas people. In other words, if we want to make our world a better place, we can start by being better.

Be someone's Barnabas. Your good deeds will eventually find their way back to you. "Therefore encourage one another and build one another up, just as you are doing." (1 Thessalonians 5:11 ESV) "Share each other's burdens, and in this way obey the law of Christ." (Galatians 6:2 NLT)

WRONGLY REJECTED

Jonathan Swift once wrote, "When a true genius appears in the world, you may know him by this sign, that the dunces are all in confederacy against him." (from *Thoughts on Various Subjects, Moral and Diverting*) Swift's pithy but pessimistic saying inspired the title of John Kennedy Toole's comedic novel, *A Confederacy of Dunces*, published in 1980—eleven years after the author committed suicide. No doubt Swift's words also described Toole's general outlook on life.

Toole's novel featured the misadventures of Ignatius J. Reilly, a well-educated but lazy 30-year-old man living with his mother in an uptown New Orleans neighborhood in the early-1960s. Walker Percy, in his introduction to the book, describes Ignatius as "a mad Oliver Hardy, a fat Don Quixote, a perverse Thomas Aquinas rolled into one." Ignatius is a dreamer who doesn't seem to fit in with the rest of the world; a man born at least a century too late, and who feels that fate is against him.

Toole had a lot in common with his literary character. Toole (December 17, 1937-March 26, 1969) was something of a scholar who lived in New Orleans with his mother well into his adulthood. And apparently he shared with his literary creation the same paranoia, the same fatalistic worldview.

Toole spiraled into a deep depression following years of rejection slips. His first novel, *The Neon Bible*, was repeatedly rejected, and the writer finally shelved the book. His next and only other novel, *A Confederacy of Dunces*, fared no better. After his countless attempts to get the book published all ended in failure, the promising young writer took his own life. He was 31.

Toole's mother, Thelma, never found the original manuscript for *Confederacy*; but one day she came across a smeared carbon copy of the novel. She wanted to see her son's book published, so she, too, tried to interest a publisher—*any* publisher—but to no avail. However, like the persistent widow of Luke 18:5, Thelma Toole refused to give up. She contacted Walker Percy, an author and college instructor at nearby Loyola University New Orleans, and asked him to read her son's manuscript. He politely refused.

But Thelma wouldn't take no for an answer. She continued to pester the instructor, now *demanding* he read it. Percy writes in his introduction:

...The lady was persistent, and it somehow came to pass that she stood in my office handing me the hefty manuscript. There was no getting out of it;

only one hope remained—that I could read a few pages and that they would be bad enough for me, in good conscience, to read no farther. ...My only fear was that this one might not be bad enough, or might be just good enough, so that I would have to keep reading. In this case I read on. And on. First with the sinking feeling that it was not bad enough to quit, then with a prickle of interest, then a growing excitement, and finally an incredulity: surely it was not possible that it was so good.

Percy recommended Toole's book to an editor at Louisiana State University Press, and *A Confederacy of Dunces* was finally published in 1980, with a print run of a mere 2,500 copies. The novel was an immediate critical and popular success, and was quickly reprinted (—and is still in print today). Ultimately the book won the Pulitzer Prize for Fiction in 1981. Was its author right? Was the world filled with dunces too blind to see his genius—and all of them arrayed against him? That's not important, really.

The lessons we truly need to take from Toole's story are about persistence...and seeking help, both emotional and practical. We've mentioned the importance of having a "barnabas" (a facilitator, or someone to help open doors of opportunity)—as well as the importance of *being* a Barnabas. Imagine how different things might have turned out if initially someone had taken the time to just read Toole's manuscript; or been there to share the author's sorrows. Toole probably would be alive today, and we'd have several more books by him.

Please take the time to see what people "are about." Don't slam the door before you even give them a chance. And if you can, *be a Barnabas!* On the other hand, if *you* feel like you've reached the end of your rope, whether due to rejections or other problems, please don't wait to reach out for help—to a doctor or a minister. The world is NOT against you! People can be callous and uncaring, but few if any actually have an agenda to keep someone from succeeding.

Above all, if you have a pessimistic, paranoid, even fatalistic outlook on life, put your focus on God. He is 100% FOR YOU. "What, then, shall we say in response to these things? If God is for us, who can be against us?" (Romans 8:31 NIV)

THE MOTHER'S DAY DREAMER

My mother was the most beautiful woman I ever saw.
All I am I owe to my mother. I attribute all my success
in life to the moral, intellectual and physical education
I received from her.

—George Washington

There's plenty of days in the year, but only one has been set aside to honor that one person in each of our lives who did the most and had the greatest impact: the ladies who carried us and nurtured us; who encouraged us to succeed, and who wiped away our tears when we failed; the women who are lovingly called MOM! For one Mother's Day, we wrote this special *Diet for Dreamers* about the lady who helped establish it as a nationally recognized holiday.

Anna Jarvis' campaign to make Mother's Day a recognized holiday in the United States began in 1905, the year her own beloved mother, Ann Reeves Jarvis, passed away. Anna's dream was to honor her mother: first, by continuing her mom's work as a peace activist— Anna's mom had cared for wounded soldiers on both sides of the American Civil War; and secondly, by creating "Mother's Day Work Clubs" to address public health issues. Anna also had a goal to establish a national holiday paying tribute to mothers throughout the country.

The FIRST modern American celebration of Mother's Day was in 1908, when Anna Jarvis held a memorial service for her mother in Grafton, West Virginia. Afterwards, due to Anna's tireless campaigning, several states officially recognized Mother's Day, with West Virginia officially recognizing the holiday in 1910. Several more states quickly followed. Ultimately, in 1914 President Woodrow Wilson signed a proclamation making Mother's Day—always to be on the second Sunday in May—a national holiday honoring mothers.

Anna had achieved her goal. Her dream to recognize and celebrate "the person who has done more for you than anyone in the world" had become a reality.

Anna Jarvis hoped the holiday would become an occasion for people to honor their own mothers and demonstrate their appreciation by writing personal letters expressing their love and gratitude. So she was actually saddened when Hallmark started marketing pre-made Mother's Day cards in early 1920. She felt the commemorative holiday she'd worked so hard to establish, was being commercialized. Perhaps. But today it's easier to be on Hallmark's side: not everyone's gifted with beautiful handwriting or the creativity to produce homemade gifts. Some of us want and need other ways to express our feelings; and besides, giving pretty cards has become as much a tradition as Mother's Day itself.

Mother's Day has since been adopted by other countries and is now celebrated all over the world. What a wonderful idea—because our moms are wonderful people!

"She is clothed with strength and dignity.... When she speaks, her words are wise, and she gives instruct-tions with kindness. She carefully watches everything in her household and suffers nothing from laziness. Her children stand and bless her." (Proverbs 31:25-28 NLT)

Join Us for a Spot of "T"?

Please excuse us, but we need to ask you a very personal question. Do you suffer from "Low T"? Ladies, STOP! Don't close this book. Don't even turn the page yet! Because *this* applies to both men and women, assuming said men and women want to fulfill their dreams!

We're not going to discuss *that* "T"—so chill out. We want to discuss another type of "T"—which empowers us to achieve our goals. If you're low in this type of "T" you'll feel sluggish and...*Ahem*...creatively impotent. Dreamer's Testosterone has three components: Timing, Talent, and Tenacity. You can lack one or two of these T's and still succeed—assuming someone "up there" is looking out for you—but you'll never get anywhere if you're deficient in all three. Which one can I do without? Which two work together best? That's something each of us will need to figure out for ourselves. You can have talent, but if the timing isn't right, or you lack tenacity, your talent won't take you very far.

Conversely, there are examples of people who had very limited talent, but who were tenacious, and who, in many cases, found themselves in the right place at the right time. Talent, tenacity, timing. You need at least one. Two's better. Have all three, and you will be a He-man (or She-woman) who can easily master the universe. Or at least make your dreams a reality.

TALENT: you either have it or you don't. But be of good cheer. It's possible to develop latent abilities and learn new skills. Often, talent is simply a glamorous word for training!

TENACITY: Just another T-word, like TRYING—only repeatedly! Try and try again! Don't allow failures or past rejections to defeat you. Get up, dust off your backside, and get back into the game. Sounds simple, but you'd be surprised how many people lack tenacity: persistence, or the ability to keep a firm grip on things when the going gets rough.

TIMING: we're cheating a little with this one. "Timing is everything!" But we often have no control over timing. Timing is like waiting to see a doctor without having an appointment: we know we have something, we know it could even spread (like our ideas), and we also know our chances of seeing the doctor are pretty good; we're just not sure if it will be during this decade. Timing, as in this case, is often out of our hands. However, we can learn to recognize good timing, by spotting trends, or studying current supply and demand, or by trying to anticipate the needs of the future.

Two Tenacious Talents with Terrific Timing!

Timing, Talent, and Tenacity are important traits for anyone pursuing a dream or a goal. Now we want to show you. Here's the story of two tenacious talents who understood good timing: Lucille Ball and Desi Arnaz.

Lucille Ball found success as the leading actress in several B movies of the 1940s. In one of these movies, she worked with a contract actor who'd soon become her husband, the Cuban-born American bandleader Desi Arnaz. Desi and Lucy married and set up housekeeping at a California ranchito they called Desilu, but they weren't able to spend much time together. By 1950, Lucy was spending most of her time in a sound booth, starring in the hit radio comedy *My Favorite Husband*. Desi was always on the road, performing at the best nightclubs. But Lucy had a plan, and she was tenacious enough to get her way.

CBS wanted to turn her popular radio show into a TV series. Television was still a relatively new medium, and Lucy doubted a weekly series could boost her career—but it could allow her more time with Desi! She agreed to do the show but with one stipulation: she demanded that Desi play her TV husband. This was anything but an easy sell: America's favorite waspy redhead married to a hot-blooded Cuban?! On a national network show?! What would the peeps out in the wheat belt have to say?! Such a thing just wasn't done! Period! But Lucy had talent AND tenacity enough to get her way. The CBS bosses relented, the peeps loved it, and the *I Love Lucy* show made television history—in more ways than one.

Turns out Desi was also a man of many talents, and just as tenacious. He wanted to film the show in Hollywood, so he and Lucy would be close to home. But again, it just wasn't done! Comedies were produced in New York, where they were broadcast live. For the West Coast audience, a video recording was made by filming the "live feed" on a program monitor, and this slightly fuzzy video, known as a kinescope, was delayed broadcast. Definitely not the best quality, but this production method was cheaper than film, and that's the way it had to be done. Period!

But Desi realized the timing was right. CBS really wanted the show. So Desi dug in his heels. He wanted the show FILMED in Hollywood using three cameras set up to capture different angles of the show as the cast performed before a live audience. The end result was more expensive, but the show looked gorgeous, and for once, the West Coast didn't have to settle for poor kinescopes. Desi's idea caught on, and soon all comedies were filmed in this manner. His talent, tenacity and ability to recognize the right timing, helped write television history.

Tune in next time, when that talented Cuban impresario realizes the timing is right for yet another innovation, one that will net him a cool million dollars in 1957! And he won't even have to work for it! We are now signing off the air!

"A man's gift makes room for him and brings him before great men." (Proverbs 18:16 NASB)

A TELEVISION MOGUL IS BORN!

We continue our topic of Talent, Tenacity and Timing—and the importance of working on these qualities if we hope to succeed. We can learn, we can practice, and we can develop talent. We can also decide to be tenacious in the pursuit of our dreams. Timing isn't always up to us, however. But we can try to spot trends and anticipate needs.

We previously mentioned the talented couple Lucille Ball and Desi Arnaz. They were tenacious, and it paid off BIG. Desi apparently also knew something about timing. He saw an opportunity as yet unrealized by just about everyone else.

Remember that Desi wanted to FILM *I Love Lucy* in Hollywood, rather than broadcast the show live from New York. The end product would be a higher quality show on FILM, a durable medium. But recording the show on film would be more expensive, and the executives at CBS were none too eager to shell out the extra funds needed to make the idea work. So Desi agreed to pay the difference with his own money. He asked that in return CBS grant him all the rights to a then unknown commodity. (What was this commodity? Be patient, we'll get to that.) At the time, Desi didn't seem to be asking for much, so the execs quickly agreed and probably left the deal rubbing their greedy little hands in glee. They'd tricked that "crazy" Cuban into footing the bill for a show that was destined to make mucho bucks for the network in sponsor's fees!

I Love Lucy premiered in 1951 to rave reviews. It was a Top 10 show, and before the first season ended the show had rocketed to the number one spot. By 1957, Desi had produced 200 episodes—on FILM. 200 hilarious, highly watchable...and re-watchable little gems sitting on the shelves at CBS. Eureka! The CBS execs got a brilliant idea! Why not rent these old episodes out to local television stations. After all, audiences loved the show *sooo* much that they'd want to catch the ones they'd missed the first time around, or just enjoy the whole show again...and again...and again. Remember, this was decades before affordable VCRs were available. And unlike today, there were no DVRs, no ON DEMAND, no $5 DVDs at Walmart. CBS was going to make a killing!!!! *Heeheehee!!!!!!*

But wait a minute—*¡Ay, caramba!*—they'd given all the rerun rights to Desi in exchange for his footing the expense of filming the show. Lucy's Latin Lover had landed them in the laundry...*er,* taken them to the cleaners!

But being both a talented actor AND businessman, Desi agreed to sell the rights back to CBS. For a cool million dollars! That's a lot of scratch for 1957! Desi used it as a down payment on the purchase of the old RKO studios, where such classics as *Citizen Kane* and *Gone with the Wind* had been produced. Desi now had at his disposal over two dozen soundstages, several back lots, and tons of camera equiment, costumes and props. (He even got Scarlett O'Hara's mansion Tara!) Everything he needed to become a television film mogul.

Lucy and Desi's dream, Desilu Studios, became a big time operation, producing such durable hits as *The Untouchables* and *Mission Impossible*...and another show that was destined to become a legend. We'll tell you about it the next article...along with the story of a talented and tenacious creator who happened to come along at just the right time!

TRY AND TRY AGAIN!

We've been discussing the three "T" traits necessary for achieving goals and fulfilling dreams. Talent is important, of course—and it can be acquired through hard work—but often it takes more than talent. Tenacity is often what counts: not giving up when repeatedly greeted by rejection, or confronted with seemingly insurmountable obstacles, or when dealing with past mistakes and failed attempts. And sometimes, it's all about the Timing.

As we mentioned in our last *Diet for Dreamers* article, Desi Arnaz seemed to be able to sense when the timing was right. But for the rest of us creators and dreamers, about the best we can do, beyond developing our talents and being tenacious, is to pray for the right timing to find us when we need it most: a door of opportunity that suddenly opens, a special need that we're uniquely suited to fill, or just a deadline that someone's desperate to meet.

Now we'll tell you about a talented and tenacious creator who might never have realized his dreams had he not stumbled upon a golden opportunity; and a legendary TV show that probably never would have made it to the air had the timing not been right.

Eugene found himself at the right place at the right time and with the right ideas. And he really needed the break. He'd been a Los Angeles cop before trying his hand at writing for television. He was good at it, too. He began writing scripts for—what else?—crime shows such as *Highway Patrol* and *Mr. District Attorney*, but he quickly graduated to other types of series, particularly westerns. In fact, he wrote 24 episodes of the popular 1950s show *Have Gun, Will Travel*. Eugene's scripts were both popular with audiences and praised by the critics. But the writer wanted more. He dreamed of creating and producing his own show.

In television, ideas for new shows are often tested before a network or cable channel makes a commitment to financially back and "air" the series. A "pilot" is ordered and produced, so TV executives can see, literally, if a concept works on film, and measure its audience appeal. During the early 1960s, Eugene continued to pitch ideas for new shows. The networks knew he was talented, so 12 times the execs gave the writer a chance to prove himself. 12 times Eugene pitched concepts for possible series. Out of all these attempts, only four of his proposals intrigued the execs enough to make it to the pilot stage.

Eugene wrote and helped produce these four pilots, but none of them were picked up for regular series. Eugene kept trying, though! (We told you he was tenacious.) And finally, he came up with an idea that made it into production! Happy ending? Not yet. Despite its popularity, his new show was cancelled at the end of its first season. You see, Eugene liked to write about controversial social issues, such as racism, and this made the TV execs nervous.

After this last failure, Eugene decided to pitch a science fiction show. If it sold, he'd be free to write about all the social ills that troubled him, because he'd simply dress up the touchy topics in Sci-fi trappings. Aliens would deal with bigotry. Wars would be protested on other planets. Audiences would get the message, but no one could be offended because Eugene wouldn't be writing about OUR SOCIETY—after all, this would be "make believe" stuff! A great idea—if it sold.

Eugene now had three big obstacles before him. He'd acquired a reputation for being a troublemaker— albeit it, a talented troublemaker. Secondly, science fiction was a tough sell in the 60s. Thirdly, there were only 3 networks in this Golden Age of TV, and two of them had already turned him down flat.

The ex-cop turned controversial writer had only one door left he could knock on. Things were not looking good for his new SF series. But a strange combination of circumstances were coming into play: a studio struggling financially, a network fighting to win the ratings race, and the marketing of the first color TV sets. Tune in next time for the conclusion of our little fable!

PRAY THEY'RE LOOKING FOR COLOR!

In the early 1960s, Desilu Studios was a force to be reckoned with. The company founded by Lucille Ball and Desi Arnaz had several hit shows and also rented out its facilities for use on many of the comedy series of the time. But by late 1962, the driving force behind Desilu was feeling the stress of running an operation with three studios, thousands of employees, dozens of busy sound stages, and acres of backlots. The joy was gone, and Desi sank into alcoholism. In the end, Desi had to walk away from it, so Lucy reluctantly took the helm.

Throughout Desilu Studios, people were nervous about the future of the company. They'd lost their captain, the creative genius who'd put Desilu on the map. And under Lucille Ball, the studio that had shined so brightly under Desi, that had produced such mega-hits as *The Untouchables*, began to lose its luster. Over the next several months, the studio released numerous ill-conceived shows which were quickly cancelled. (Remember the series *Glynis*? Neither do we.) This string of failures resulted in Desilu losing tons of money.

Over at CBS, the network that had profited handsomely from the success of the *I Love Lucy* show, was watching Desilu's steady decline with horror. William

Paley, the head of the network, was a big fan of Lucille Ball's work, and he also felt indebted to her studio. So he sent two of his best men—troubleshooters—to fix Desilu. One was a financial expert, the other a savvy Jewish programming executive named Herbert Solow.

Solow arrived with one objective: help Desilu develop some viable series that would get the studio back in the game. To accomplish this task, he needed to find high concept projects that would stand out from the typical TV fare of westerns and cop shows. He quickly found two projects that fit the bill: an unusual spy show called *Mission: Impossible* (ironically, also an apt description for Solow's assignment at Desilu) which would become iconic; and an SF series pitched by an L.A. cop who'd found critical success as a writer.

You remember Eugene? We last left the controversial writer and producer struggling to sell his SF series. He'd recently become something of a hot potato for wanting to write about important social issues. Plus, SF was not an easy sell at the time. But fortunately for Eugene, Desilu—now under the guiding hand of Solow—was looking for unusual projects, and had better things to do than be upset by a little controversy. In other words, when the talented and tenacious writer approached Solow, the timing was right. (Actually, it was perfect!)

Solow later described the ex-cop turned writer as a "mumbling exotic" who appeared to have "recently learned to dress himself but hadn't yet quite gotten the knack." A slightly disheveled Eugene handed Solow a wrinkled sheet of paper with his concept for a new series. Solow overlooked all this, because he saw the potential in both the writer and his ideas. He quickly grabbed the show for production at Desilu, but Solow still needed to secure a network to televise the series. Here's where Solow had his work cut out.

Remember, Eugene had a reputation for being trouble, and at the time, SF was "alien" to the network money men. Not to mention, the "mumbling" writer was terrible at making a presentation. The first two times Eugene had pitched the series to network executives, Solow hadn't been present; and the results had been disastrous: two of the three major networks had already passed on his show. DEFINITELY NOT GOOD!! This was, after all, an extremely primitive age long before the advent of multiple cable channels, and Solow knew they had only one chance left of selling the series, to the "peacock" network (NBC)—and he wasn't about to let anything screw it up.

Solo essentially dressed and groomed Eugene for the presentation; he told him exactly what to say and how to say it; and he told him when to just keep his mouth shut. When the two men arrived at NBC the timing was again PERFECT. The network wanted to return to the number one spot in the ratings, which they had previously occupied; but they couldn't get there with all the musical and comedy variety shows currently proliferating their schedule. They were ready for bold new ideas. They wanted unusual and COLORFUL shows, which is why they'd already scheduled *I-Spy* starring TV's first African-American superstar, Bill Cosby!

NBC grabbed the series, but not just because it sounded like an awesome show. NBC was owned by RCA, the corporation at the forefront of color television technology. RCA wanted NBC to air more shows "in Living Color" in order to boost the sales of color TV sets; and Solow promised NBC that Eugene's new show would be filmed in LIVING COLOR! So, again, the timing was right. However, years later an NBC executive commented, "It was Herb's tenacity and presentation that sold the series." (Herb, by the way, was a "Barnabas.")

Eugene (Gene) Roddenberry's cultural phenomenon *STAR TREK* probably never would have seen the light of day were it not for Solow's tenacity and some really good timing! Moral: be tenacious, ask God to open the perfect door in His perfect TIMING—*heh,* and pray they're looking for color!

"God never changes His mind when He gives gifts or when He calls someone." (Romans 11:29 GOD'S WORD)

A RECORD OF FAILURE?

He was an American author who penned 55 novels, 83 short stories, over 200 poems and numerous movie scripts. The inventiveness of his Victorian-era fiction anticipated gadgets and trends that were decades away, such as television, laptop computers, wireless phones, and women in dangerous occupations. But mostly Lyman Baum was known for two things: his many children's books; and his failure at just about every venture he tried before writing.

Lyman was born on May 15, 1856, in New York, into a prosperous and devout Methodist family. Lyman never cared for the name his father gave him, and instead went by his middle name, Frank. As a child he suffered from poor health and was tutored at home. He turned his interests to several creative pursuits such as writing. When he was 11, Lyman's father purchased him a cheap printing press, and the boy spent many hours publishing thin journals and catalogs, mainly about stamp collecting.

When he was 20, Lyman took up poultry breeding, which at the time was a national craze. And although he published a monthly trade journal, *The Poultry Record*, and later wrote a book on the subject, the venture otherwise failed.

For a while, Lyman worked in his brother's dry goods store, but he was drawn to acting and the stage. In 1880, his father built him a theatre in Richburg, New York, and Lyman quickly wrote several plays, and assembled a stage company to perform his work. But while he was touring with the company, his theatre caught fire and burned to the ground, consuming all the props, costumes, and the only known copies of several of Lyman's scripts.

In July 1888, Lyman and his wife moved to the Dakota Territory, where he opened a store that specialized in upscale merchandise. It was a very bad idea. Lyman was not a savvy businessman, and Baum's Bazaar quickly went bankrupt. Lyman then turned to editing a local newspaper, *The Aberdeen Saturday Pioneer*, for which he wrote an often controversial column. The paper went under. The column went with it.

Failed chicken farmer, failed theatre manager, failed shop owner, failed newspaperman. It was time to try something else. So, at the age of 44, Lyman finally pursued one of his first loves, writing. First up, an unusual children's novel based on whimsical stories he frequently shared with the neighboring kids. He finished *The Emerald City* on October 9, 1899. It was rejected so many times by so many publishers that Lyman kept a journal of all the rejection letters he received. He called it "A Record of Failure"!

One editor stated the book is "Too radical of a departure from traditional juvenile literature." Lyman persevered, however, and found a publisher willing to print a modest run of 10,000 copies in January 1901. Within less than six months not only had the first printing sold out, but a second printing of 15,000 copies also was close to being depleted.

Since that time, L. Frank Baum's *The Wonderful Wizard of Oz* has sold over 15 million copies. The novel and its 13 sequels have been adapted into numerous movies, stage plays, and comics; and the wondrous Land of Oz continues to capture the imaginations of children of all ages. Not a bad finish to Lyman's track record of failure!

"...But this one thing I do, forgetting those things which are behind and extending myself unto those things which are ahead, I press toward the mark for the prize of the high calling of God in Christ Jesus." (Philippians 3:13 Jubilee Bible 2000)

Close Shave

with the Critics!

In 1782, Giovanni Paisiello composed an Italian comic opera based on the 1775 French comedy *The Barber of Seville*. The work was extremely popular with both audiences and critics, who hailed it as a triumph. For over three decades Paisiello's opera was considered the definitive version of The Barber. Then, in 1815, Gioachino Rossini composed a new and very different version of the same comedy. Rossini's opera met with incredible resistance. Paisiello wasn't at all pleased to hear of this new version, and neither were his legions of fans! Just who did this upstart Rossini think he was?

Rossini's version premiered on February 20, 1816, at the Teatro Argentina in Rome. When the young composer arrived for the performance he was greeted by an angry mob. His associates hustled Rossini into the theater where, a short time later, an audience composed mostly of Paisiello's passionate and vocal supporters jeered and hissed throughout the performance. Not only was Rossini's *Barber of Seville* a total failure, but also, before it was over, several onstage accidents had occurred.

Undaunted, the composer arrived a few days later for a second performance. On that fateful day, Rossini was again hurried through the mob. The audience was quieter, and the performance went far more smoothly, but afterwards, when Rossini left the theater through a back entrance, he was met by the same mob as before. Only this time, his entourage failed to keep away the crowd. Yes, the mob closed in and the next thing Rossini knew he'd been dragged off his feet. A moment later he found himself hoisted up...and carried atop the hysterical crowd, as the people paraded their new operatic hero upon their shoulders through the streets, praising the name *ROSSINI!!*

Today, few remember the name or work of Paisiello; but Rossini's *Barber of Seville* has endured as one of the greatest masterpieces of comedy within music. Even more than two centuries later, its popularity on the modern opera stage attests to its greatness.

We all know the expression "That's a hard act to follow"; but if you're a performer, musician, or writer, and you're following in the footsteps of someone who's famous and successful; or if you're simply trying something new and different, take heart. Many times the naysayers know nothing!

When director Tim Burton announced that the comedic actor Michael Keaton would be playing Batman in the 1989 movie, fans gasped. "Are you kidding! 'Mr. Mom' can't be Batman! He'll ruin the movie!" Well, Burton was doing something different, and his film was a box-office bonanza. So how did Keaton manage in a darker role? Just fine. And he even returned for a sequel. In fact, when Keaton moved on and Warners recast the part, the fans lamented.

Nearly two decades later, Warners decided to reboot the franchise, and its new director, Christopher Nolan, announced that Welsh actor Christian Bale would be playing Batman. "You can't be serious!" the fans yelled. "The sicko from *American Psycho* is going to play our hero?" *Hey, come on!* That's why they're actors. Bale's portrayal is now considered by most fans to be the definitive Batman, and after three movies it'll be tough getting used to another actor in the role. Ben Affleck has his work cut out in the fourth incarnation of the character, but we've learned it doesn't always pay to be a naysayer.

Someone once said, and it may even have been Steven Spielberg, that Harrison Ford is too well known as the space pirate Han Solo from his Star Wars movies; and that he'll never be able to convince audiences that he's the adventurous straight-arrow archeologist Indiana Jones. In fact, the part almost went to Tom Selleck, who bowed out at the last minute to continue starring in *Magnum P.I.* But after *Raiders of the Lost Ark* and its three sequels...well, Ford obviously proved any naysayers wrong. Do you have any naysayers in your life? Persevere! And prove them wrong!

KEEP FIGHTING
THE GOOD FIGHT!

U.S. President and "Rough Rider" Teddy Roosevelt once stated, "There is no effort without error or shortcoming"! This is one of the great, unchangeable facts of Life. Furthermore, if you're making mistakes—if you frequently stumble and fall—then you're probably on the right track, trying new things, aiming for higher goals. Failure is no fun, but it's usually the first step to achieving something worthwhile.

We know this truth. Deep down, YOU also probably know this. And God certainly knows it! Which is why He encourages us to keep on trying, to keep on fighting the good fight of faith. When we fail, He admonishes us to get up.

Elvis Presley was fired from the Grand Ole Opry in 1954, after giving one performance. The house manager told Elvis, "You ain't goin' nowhere, son. You ought to go back to drivin' a truck."

Before he succeeded, Henry Ford, the founder of the Ford Motor Company, failed and went broke five times! And R. H. Macy failed seven times before his New York City department store caught on.

Fred Smith turned in a college paper about his concept for a reliable overnight delivery service. His Yale professor gave the paper a "C" and told him, "...Your concept is interesting and well formed, but...your ideas also have to be feasible." Smith went on to found Federal Express.

Throughout his life Thomas Alva Edison, "The Wizard of Menlo Park," was a glorious "failure"! As a child, his teachers sent him home one day, stating the boy is "too stupid to learn anything." As a young adult, Edison seemed to be proving his teachers right. He was fired from his first two jobs for being "non-productive." Can this possibly be the same tireless American inventor who held 1,093 U.S. patents in his name? Yes. What set Edison apart was his determination. He refused to quit, and he viewed every failure as taking a step closer to succeeding. Which is why Edison continued to "fail"!

Although Edison did NOT invent the light bulb, he did invent a way to make the idea feasible. The bulbs of previous inventors were bulky, expensive, and consumed too much power. Edison wanted to produce an economical, more energy efficient bulb using low-cost materials. He tried a thousand different material combinations, which all failed, before finding the right one. When a reporter asked him, "How did it feel to fail 1,000 times?" Edison replied, "I didn't fail 1,000 times. The light bulb was an invention with 1,000 steps."

Failure is the foundation upon which we build success. Nehemiah 13:2 is one of several scriptures that demonstrate how God is able to turn every curse into a blessing. Also, "...God causes everything to work together for the good of those who love God and are called according to his purpose for them." (Romans 8:28 NLT)

We crawl before we walk. We walk before we run. We learn by doing, and we learn our best lessons from our mistakes. Yes, we'd always prefer to get it right the first time, but our failures are NOT the end of the line, they are stepping stones on the path to success—unless we stop trying. Please don't. Edison once stated, "Many of life's failures are people who did not realize how close they were to success when they gave up."

And if you don't occasionally fail, then you're probably not continuing to raise the bar on what you can accomplish. So keep on slugging. "Fight the good fight of faith; take hold of the eternal life...." (Timothy 6:12 NASB) "My flesh and my heart may fail, but God is the strength of my heart and my portion forever." (Psalm 73:26 ESV)

AN INVINCIBLE DREAM!

This is the story of two Jewish kids, Joseph and Jerome. Joe was born in Canada. His father had emigrated there from Rotterdam and opened a tailor shop in Toronto's garment district. His mother had come from Kiev in the Ukraine.

When he was about eight or nine years old, Joe got a job selling newspapers to help support his family. He would also scrounge around for scraps of paper— anything with some blank space on it, like the backs of discarded handbills, shreds of unused wallpaper— whatever he could get his hands on. Joe dreamed of someday becoming an artist, but he needed drawing paper.

In 1924, Joe's family moved to Cleveland, Ohio, where Joe started attending Glenville High School. Joe was painfully shy and had trouble making friends, until he met Jerry—just another shy Jewish kid with big dreams. Jerry once said, "When Joe and I first met, it was like the right chemicals coming together."

Jerry, the youngest of six children, was a Cleveland native. His dad had emigrated from Lithuania, and opened a haberdashery. America in the 1920s was indeed a land of opportunity—but it was not without its share of problems: in 1932, while Jerry was in junior high, his father's shop was robbed. Reeling from the shock and the resultant loss of the crime, Jerry's father suffered a fatal heart attack.

A year later, Jerry met Joe. Two shy dreamers, both sons of immigrants, both struggling with adversity, both trying to fit in. These two Jewish loners discovered they had similar interests and similar goals. They both found escape in the popular adventure movies and science fiction magazines of the day, which featured stars like the dashing Douglas Fairbanks, Sr., and heroes such as Doc Savage and Flash Gordon. And together they wanted to write and draw the same kinds of stories that so thrilled them. That's right, a couple of depression-era geeks.

Joe and Jerry hung out together, dreamed together, and created together! They were closer than brothers. They were the two sides of a single coin. And together, Joe and Jerry came up with a brilliant idea for a new heroic character. There had never been anything like it. The two young men knew the idea couldn't miss. Or could it?! Often, timing is everything. Was the world ready for something different? Probably so. Were the publishers ready? Not yet.

A primitive first version of the character appeared in 1933, in a short story published in a science fiction fan-magazine produced by Jerry. A few months later, he and Joe refined the character, produced a new illustrated story, and started looking for a real publisher. Then came the rejections, the closed doors, the don't-call-us-we'll-call-you disappointments. Four long years of NO!

The two friends had knocked on the doors of every publishing company, every newspaper syndicate, and not a single editor or publisher wanted their story or saw the potential of their fictional character. At one point, Joe the artist got so discouraged that he burned all the pages of the story; with Jerry the writer managing to rescue only the cover from the fire.

Things looked bleak for their new hero. And Joe and Jerry's future was starting to dim. They shelved their idea and moved on to other things. Both men finally found work with various magazines, doing the things they loved: Jerry wrote; Joe illustrated. They were content—mostly. They had overcome social and economic adversity, and at a time just a few years after the Great Depression, they were actually being paid to create fiction and artwork. But Joe and Jerry continued to dream of their forgotten hero and all the fun and adventure they could have shared with the world. Little did they know the fate awaiting both them and their idea for a bold, new character, little could they imagine that their work would continue to influence and shape pop culture for the next eight decades, or that their names would feature prominently in the media of the then distant 21st century. Little could they comprehend that theirs was an invincible dream that would not die!

To Be Continued:

Join us next time, when we witness the fate awaiting our heroes Joe and Jerry, as they continue their battle against the forces of adversity! Don't miss Chapter 2 of AN INVINCIBLE DREAM!

AN INVINCIBLE DREAM!

CHAPTER 2

Last episode: Joe and Jerry were just two Jewish kids who loved science fiction and adventure pulps. Both boys were sons of immigrants, both had overcome social and economic adversity, both dreamed of better things. After they met in a Cleveland high school, they began to hang out together, dream together, and create together! And together, Joe and Jerry came up with a brilliant idea for a new heroic character. There had never been anything like it. The two young men knew the idea couldn't miss. Or could it?!

Joe and Jerry modeled their new science fiction character after the Old Testament hero Samson, and decided to make him an alien being trying to fit in to life on earth—because that's what they themselves felt like in America, strangers in a strange land. And, like the story of Moses, their character's mother would place her baby in a vessel that his father would launch into the river of space. The vessel would find its way to earth, where this extremely foreign child would grow up. He would live among us, blessing us with his special talents; but he could never be one of us. Even though he looked identical to humans, he would never actually feel like one. He'd never be able to forget he was an alien.

We said America was a land of opportunity, didn't we? Originally, Joe and Jerry got the idea to market the hero as a comic strip for daily newspapers. They showed their ideas to an editor named Max Gaines. Gaines wasn't interested. Then the boys approached several newspaper syndicates, none of which were interested in running a strip featuring their hero. So Joe and Jerry finally threw in the towel. They put away their story samples and started working on other things.

During the mid-thirties, something very American and very Jewish was beginning to captivate readers: comic books—which were mostly reprints of the Sunday "Funnies." By 1938, magazine publishers began to fully realize the profitability of the form. One such publisher decided to start up a comics magazine featuring all new material. Word got around to Gaines, who apparently hadn't forgotten young Joe and Jerry. He contacted all the right people, and Joe and Jerry's comic strip, reformatted as comic-book pages, was published in July 1938 as the cover story in the first issue of a new magazine.

The hero created by two Jewish boys was an immediate hit. The character literally took off. Other publishers quickly copied him, and a lucrative new entertainment genre was born. A year later Joe and Jerry's hero got his own comic book, with his name as the title (a first for comics). The next year a popular radio show premiered. It was almost immediately followed, in 1941, by a series of high-quality animated shorts that played before feature films. Eventually, the character got the live-action treatment, in a 1948 movie serial. All these appearances of the character were hugely successful.

In 1952, Joe and Jerry's creation burst into television! The show was such a hit that people went out and purchased TV sets just so they could see it. There were lunch boxes, toys, games, and costumes. The trend of licensing a character for tie-in merchandise started with this character, and it changed the face of marketing. There were more cartoons and trading cards, and finally, in 1978, the character received the big-budget motion picture treatment. The movie cleaned up at the box office, and was followed by three sequels and another TV series.

Still another weekly series premiered in 2001 and ran for ten years. And in 2013, the most expensive movie version yet, premiered to legions of excited fans. It made $668 million worldwide, and its sequel, arriving in 2016, is one of the most discussed and anticipated movies in years. Have you figured out who we're talking about yet?

Today, Jerry Siegel and Joe Shuster's Superman is one of the most recognizable characters in the world. He's credited with jumpstarting an art form that has evolved into a multi-billion dollar industry. If not for the success of Superman, there'd be no Batman or Captain America or Spiderman. And the movie industry would have lost the source material for several of its highest grossing films. In fact, movie versions of comic books (we call them graphic novels these days) have helped to invigorate Hollywood—just as Superman invigorated comics. It's quite possible Superman is the most important fictional character ever created, the match that lit the fuse that ignited an entire industry—several industries, actually. But it almost didn't happen!

Superman almost succumbed to the kryptonite of rejection!

"Write the vision; make it plain...For still the vision awaits its appointed time; ...If it seems slow, wait for it; it will surely come...." (Habakkuk 2:2-3 ESV)

WAIT FOR IT!

Most of us know that when it comes to fulfilling dreams, opportunity arrives in its own sweet time, and success can take years to achieve. So we wait for it...patiently. But waiting is never passive. Waiting is a process. Waiting requires us to exercise our faith, to be expectant, to be watchful.

We need to spend whatever time it takes (to achieve our goals) studying, training, practicing and preparing. Waiting allows us the time necessary to get ready. Waiting on a dream to come true is like waiting on a meal. Waiting helps us to work up a hearty appetite. We can smell success in the air, we hunger for it. We work harder and more diligently to prepare that "meal." And when we finally get to sit down and eat it, we realize we enjoy it a lot more. For obvious reasons it tastes better and we appreciate it far more.

We absolutely LOVE pizza. Good New York-style pizza! We frequent a fantastic Italian restaurant where the waiters speak in broken English, and the pizza is delicious. But when we're really hungry, as in practically starving after a long day of running errands, it's like manna from heaven, food of the gods—something that was truly worth waiting for.

Okay, sometimes "Whatever time it takes" feels like eternity. Why, oh why are we having to wait *soooo* long.

Hey, however long the process takes, whether we wait a year or 30 years, it's going to feel too long. Like time itself, waiting is relative. Just ask Einstein. The secret to waiting is knowing that God's timing is perfect. He knows exactly when and how we need to succeed. Remembering this fact is the key to NOT gOIng CRazY!

"There is an appointed time for everything. And there is a time for every event under heaven—" (Ecclesiastes 3:1 NASB)

We can personally testify that waiting is never easy! And although it's an unsettling truth, people sometimes have to wait years, even decades, to see their dreams come true. Now there's an uncomfortable thought none of us want to entertain. But what if you should have to wait a long, long, LONG time to achieve your goals? What will you do? Will you grow impatient? Will you even consider giving up?

We hope not! Winston Churchill once said, "Never, never, never give up." And he never did! But we still need to face the cold hard facts of life: some dreams take longer, and some people work years to achieve their goals. We mention this NOT to push you over the edge of depression, but rather to encourage you! To motivate you not to give up. Waiting is hard, but it can also be productive. As we stated previously, spend the time getting ready—or, depending on how long you've been waiting—getting ready-*er!*

Learn to trust God while you're waiting. And work up an appetite! "...They that wait upon the LORD shall renew their strength; they shall mount up with wings as eagles; they shall run, and not be weary; and they shall walk, and not faint." (Isaiah 40:31 KJB)

GERIATRIC GIANT-SLAYERS!

We've stated that waiting for opportunity's knock is a process during which we need to prepare and learn to trust God. We also pointed out that although God's timing is perfect, we sometimes need to face the unsettling truth that some dreams take a very long time. We don't give up, though! We keep waiting. But exactly how long do we wait? Simple answer: as long as it takes. But what if I grow old while waiting? Complex answer: first, age (and the concept of "old") is relative. What you think is old might be young to us; and what you consider young may seem old to others. God doesn't seem to take age into consideration when working in people's lives, so neither should we. Besides, if you're still kicking, you're not too old to fulfill your dreams.

You think we're being optimistic. Well, we are. But what can be gained by being pessimistic? Nada. Plus, we have some great examples of people who seemed way too old to fulfill their dreams, but who in fact weren't! That is, they WERE old—no doubt about it—but not too old to achieve their goals.

First up: the Biblical Patriarch Abraham and his wife Sarah wanted a son. A son, in the Hebrew culture, represented the future: a male heir to continue the family name and tradition. So this couple's dream was to leave a legacy; and they had good reason to believe their dream would someday come true, because God had actually promised Abraham it would; that he'd have a son and, through that son, leave an incredible legacy. Okay, have a son, big deal. Well, it was a big deal, because Sarah couldn't seem to bear children.

Abraham and Sarah waited for the promise to be fulfilled. And then they waited some more. Each morning, the same thing—no, not today. Oh, and uh, tomorrow's not looking too good, either. But they trusted God, and continued to wait...for years and years! While they waited, they continued to work and prepare for their future, always trusting and staying faithful to God. How many of us could do that? Only Abraham, which is why the Bible regards him as the Father of Faith.

But even Abraham was beginning to wonder *WHEN?!?* the promise was going to be fulfilled. After all, he was 99 years old, and his wife was so far past the age of childbearing that things now looked scientifically impossible. Then one day, God simply announced, "It's time!" Actually, the Bible states, "...Sarah conceived and bore a son to Abraham in his old age, at the appointed time...." (Genesis 21:2 NASB) Two major things you need to take away from this piece of history: first, God fulfilled the promise in an "appointed time"! God had a plan and His plan was perfect! And His timing was perfect, too! (Remember this, while you're waiting.) God needed to get Abraham to a certain place at a certain time and with certain life experiences. Second, God's perfect timing came when Abraham and Sarah were—in the eyes of those around them—as old as spit! In God's eyes, however, they weren't too old. With God, age is a question of mind over matter. If you don't mind, it don't matter!

It certainly didn't matter to Caleb! He was one of the twelve spies sent to reconnoiter the Promised Land.

Do you have a promised land? A place or level you want to be? Caleb and Joshua returned from their promised land to tell Moses that there were giants standing between them and where they wanted to be. Caleb and Joshua wanted to go back immediately and slay those giants, but the other ten, pessimistic and spineless spies convinced the people to stay where they were—in the wilderness.

45 years later, Caleb finally got his opportunity to slay the giants! Once the Hebrews entered and began taking their promised land, there remained one terrifying territory where a formidable race of giants still walked the earth. These giants lived in great fortified cities positioned atop several hills. Now, if you know anything about military strategy, you know it's harder to take out an enemy entrenched on the high ground, let alone giant enemies behind fortified battlements. But Caleb went to his old friend Joshua, and said, "...Give me this hill country (promised by the Lord)...and I shall drive them out...." (Joshua 14:12 NASB)

Joshua consented, so at the age of 85, Caleb set out to take his own, personal promised land. Caleb, the geriatric giant-slayer, wasn't about to let anything stand in the way of his dream, not giants, not naysayers, not old age!

"But as for me, I trust in You, O Lord. You are my God. My times are in Your hand." (Psalm 31:14-15)

Seriously Seasoned
Superstars!

Your old men will dream dreams,
And your young men will see visions.
                                    —Joel 2:28 NLT

When we continue to work hard and dream big, our greatest successes can often come later in life. In "Geriatric Giant-Slayers," we examined the lives of two men of the Bible, who achieved their dreams at ripe old ages—proving you're never too gray to achieve your goals. We also discussed how age is relative. We've met people who are seventy and eighty-something, but who are real go-getters; and forty-year-olds who act like life is over. No matter how OLD you think you are, please don't retire to the rocker just yet. Keep on dreaming and creating. We now hope to inspire you with the examples of two modern-day Geriatric Giant-Slayers:

The award-winning actor Morgan Freeman didn't simply burst onto the big screen; his fame and universally recognized voice and image are the culmination of years of hard work and perseverance, and it arrived much later in his life. First off, Freeman never actually planned to be an actor. He served four years in the U.S. Air Force as a mechanic before the acting bug bit. Then came years of small parts on the stage, leading to starring roles on the stage, leading to bit parts in television, leading to bigger and better things in several made-for-TV movies. Had he arrived? Not yet.

Freeman was destined to play Frederick Douglass, Thurgood Marshall, Nelson Mandela and GOD!! (And it was good.) Not to mention the brains who kept Batman fully equipped in three box-office bonanzas. But getting these plum assignments meant working several more years, in supporting roles—*Sigh, again?*—in smaller theatrical movies.

Finally, in 1989, Freeman wowed us in unforgettable roles in two big-budget movies, *Glory!* and *Driving Miss Daisy.* He'd really hit the big time, and he was only 52! Today, at age 77, Freeman is spending his remaining golden years gentling rocking—as senators, scientists, doctors and diplomats—in an average of four movies a year! In fact, he's one of the busiest actors in Hollywood! Didn't you get the memo?

Another late bloomer: Patrick O'Brian worked decades as a novelist but didn't become more widely read and better known until he was in his late sixties. Suddenly his series of novels set during the Napoleonic Wars and featuring British Naval Captain Jack Aubrey and Ship's Doctor and sometimes intelligence agent Stephen Maturin, were making the *New York Times* Bestsellers List. Walter Cronkite and Charlton Heston were among his avid readers, and after 20 engaging novels, as well as numerous Patrick O'Brian interviews and speaking engagements, a big-budget movie based on two of the books was filmed: *Master and Commander: The Far Side of the World*, starring Russell Crowe and Paul Bettany.

So you're never too old to reach new heights. You're never too old to dream, create, achieve your goals, and live life to the fullest!

"I will be your God throughout your lifetime—until your hair is white with age. I made you, and I will care for you." (Isaiah 46:4 NLT)

POPCORN, PASSION & PETROL!

The road to success is often long and bumpy. The journey necessary to fulfill dreams or achieve goals can take years. Many people start out on their "quest" strong and full of hope. But somewhere along the way, long before they arrive at that special place they desire to be, whether it's a level of skill or scholarship, a career position or an accomplishment, they run out of steam. Like a car that's out of gas, they begin to coast; their progress slows, their enthusiasm wanes, until eventually they pull off to the side of the road, often just a few "miles" short of their destination.

As these people stand next to their stalled dreams, others speed past them—all the way to the finish line. Why do some give up when they're so close? What enables others to complete the journey? Simple. The ones who don't make it, who give up and stop moving forward, failed to refuel. Those who made it all the way not only refueled, but they also had the *right* fuel. Faith is one such fuel, which we explore in the next chapter; and there are others worth listing, but today however, we discuss just one...with an encouraging success story.

We may be tempted to think of the late Orville Redenbacher as the goofy-looking guy in horn-rimmed glasses and nerdy bowtie who pitched popcorn on television for several decades. But he was anything but goofy. The glasses and bowtie were affectations he adopted for his TV ads. This prosperous popcorn patriarch had both business savvy and the determination not to quit. He also had the right fuel needed to make it all the way to the top of the popcorn heap. High test gas. Premium petrol. Rocket fuel. Redenbacher was passionate: he had an enthusiasm, a zeal, a fervor, a preoccupation—perhaps even a mania—regarding one single thing. He had a passion for popcorn that began early and lasted to the end. It fueled his tenacity and ultimately his success.

Redenbacher was born in Indiana, July 16, 1907, and grew up on his family's farm, helping out with assorted chores. As a teenager he'd finish his work early so he'd have time to work at his side business, selling—what else?—popcorn from the back of his car. When he graduated from high school he was in the top 5% of his class. He then attended Purdue University, where he ran track and performed in the Purdue All-American Marching Band. In 1928, he graduated with a degree in agronomy, the science of soil management and crop production. His obsession with popcorn was far from over. And he'd trained for it.

Redenbacher spent most of his life in the agriculture industry. He served as a Farm Bureau extension agent, and even sold fertilizer, but popcorn was never far from his thoughts. In his spare time he continued to dabble with the food and, in 1951, he and friend Charlie Bowman purchased an Indiana seed corn plant. Over the next twenty years, the two men experimented with tens of thousands of hybrid strains of popcorn. They eventually settled on one they named "RedBow," which had all the perfect popcorn qualities they'd long sought.

In 1970, when Redenbacher was 63, the two entrepreneurs finally launched their popping corn. Orville hit the road as the official pitchman, appearing on talk shows and in commercials. By the mid-1970s, Redenbacher and Bowman had captured a third of the un-popped popcorn market. The rest is food history, but clearly, Redenbacher's passion for popcorn sufficiently fueled him for a journey to success that took about fifty years—from selling it out of the trunk of his car, to pitching it on national television.

Are you passionate about your dreams? If not, you may wish to ask yourself why. Passion can keep you on track. Passion keeps you going when the road gets bumpy. Passion helps you make it all the way to the finish. And if you're NOT passionate about something, is it really worth pursuing? For the long haul? If you believe it is, then get passionate about it. Otherwise, discover your passion in life, and start pursuing that instead.

Passion is a vital fuel for the journey. "Do you not know that in a race all the runners run, but only one receives the prize? So run that you may obtain it." (1 Corinthians 9:24 ESV)

FUELED BY FAITH!

The journey to fulfill your dreams or achieve your goals can take years. Many people start out strong and full of hope, but somewhere along the way—sometimes just short of reaching their goals—they run out of steam and give up on the journey. These people often abandon their stalled dreams, like a car that's run out of gas, as others speed past them—all the way to the finish line. We recently began discussing reasons why some give up when they're so close; and what enables others to complete the journey. It all boils down to a few things.

If you're going to achieve your goals, fulfill your dreams, reach your desired destination, you'll need to:

(1) *Stay on course* —no veering, no side stops. Stay focused on your objectives in life. If circumstances such as time, money, health, or family obligations force you to take a detour, make every effort to get back on track as soon as possible. Detours in life happen. But detours should be just that: round about ways and slightly longer routes that eventually get us THERE! No one ever intentionally takes a detour and then decides not to get back on the main road...unless they don't have enough fuel in their tanks.

(2) *Fuel up!* The fuel we discussed last time is PASSION: an enthusiasm, a zeal, a fervor, a preoccupation—perhaps even a mania—for what you're hoping to achieve. But there's another, even more important fuel: FAITH. Believe it or not, everybody has faith—in something! If not, no one would ever have the courage to get into a car and go out on the freeway during rush hour. Now THAT'S faith in action: faith in God, faith in the car's proper functioning, faith in the driver, faith in all the other drivers. People only differ in what they have faith IN. The atheists have faith in science. They don't believe in a supreme God who created the Universe and all that's in it, including people; or that God is still in control and that He cares about us.

Some people put their faith in themselves. What a shock these people must get, when they try something and fail. And sooner or later we all fail and come up short—repeatedly. The great Patriarch Abraham chose to put his faith in the Judeo-Christian God of the Bible. And it was his faith in God that kept him fueled on his long, sometimes winding journey to reach his destiny.

Abraham was so gassed up with premium fuel that the Bible refers to him as the "Father of Faith"; not because he was perfect—no, Abraham was far from perfect—but he WAS faithful! When God asked his friend Abraham to do something, he did it.

God made Abraham a promise: that he would one day have a son, and through that son Abraham would leave a legacy to all the world. So Abraham's dream was to see the promise fulfilled, and reach his destiny. There were, however, two huge roadblocks. First, try as she might, Abraham's wife Sarah had been unable to bear a child, and now she was so far past the age of childbearing that things were looking scientifically impossible. Second, the journey to the promise took not years but rather DECADES. So Abraham needed to stay fueled, if he was to stay the course, and obtain the promise. Did he make it to the finish line? Did he and Sarah receive the Son of Promise? Yup. After a quarter-century he reached his goal!! And you can read about it in the historical book of Genesis, chapters 18 and 20.

"Abraham never wavered in believing God's promise. In fact, his faith grew stronger, and in this he brought glory to God. He was fully convinced that God is able to do whatever he promises." (Romans 4:20-21 NLT) "It was by faith that even Sarah was able to have a child, though she was barren and was too old. She believed that God would keep his promise." (Hebrews 11:11 NLT)

Sooner or later, we all need a little help in life. We have to put our confidence, our trust, in something greater than ourselves. We've put our trust in the God of Abraham, Isaac and Israel. We hope you have, too. "Now all glory to God, who is able, through his mighty power at work within us, to accomplish infinitely more than we might ask or think." (Ephesians 3:20 NLT)

Next we'll explore what faith is and how to keep your tank full. Happy motoring!

THE FACTS OF FAITH

The journey to accomplishing your goals, fulfilling your dreams, or receiving a promise, can take years. Many people start out strong, but somewhere along the way—often just short of the finish line—they run out of steam and give up. If you're going to achieve your goals, and reach your desired destination, you'll need to: (1) stay on course—no veering, no side stops (stay focused on your main objectives); and (2) stay fueled by faith, the premium "gas" that enables you to complete your journey. But what exactly is FAITH, anyway?

Faith is an unshakeable belief or confidence in something or someone. If Michael Jordan ever told his teammates he wasn't sure he could make a particular shot from the free throw line, they probably smiled and said something like: "We KNOW you can make this free throw! We have FAITH in you!" Jordan's teammates had seen "His Airness" in action, and they had complete confidence in his ability to slam dunk the basketball. Putting our complete confidence in God isn't too different. Many of us have seen the God of Creation do some pretty amazing things. And really, we can daily see His mighty hand in the flight of a hummingbird, in the smile of a child...in life itself. For others, including those individuals too myopic to see the everyday miracles taking place all around them, there's an historical document recording the greatest feats and most glorious triumphs of all time—all performed by the all-powerful, all-knowing God of Abraham, Isaac, and Israel—and it's called the Bible (literally, THE book)! All we need do is read it!

Seeing is believing, right? But true Faith is still believing even when we can't see. That takes an incredible amount of TRUST. We believe in the human soul, but we can't see it or measure its physical dimensions. We also believe in an invisible God. And we believe in His divine ability to freely grant us eternal life.

Jesus Christ—after returning from the dead, a fact verified by reliable contemporary witnesses—told His disciples, "You believe because you have seen me. Blessed are those who believe without seeing me." (John 20:29 NLT) "In the same way, Abraham believed God, and God counted him as righteous because of his faith. The real children of Abraham [the Father of our Faith], then, are those who put their faith in God." (Galatians 3:6-7 NLT)

How does the Bible define Faith? "...Faith is confidence in what we hope for and assurance about what we do not see. This is what the ancients were commended for." (Hebrews 11:1 NIV) So, you can imagine how important faith is for fueling our dreams and all those invisible goals we hope to achieve. Another translation states it this way: "...Faith is...the conviction of things not seen." (NASB) Do you have any strong convictions? About issues or ideals? Or about certain incidents? Here's an example: "I'm absolutely positive that Junior broke the cookie jar—even if I wasn't there to see it happen."

One last translation: "...Faith is the reality of what is hoped for...." (Holman CSB) Faith is confidence or conviction or—*in this sense*—treating something as though it were a "done deal." Children do this all the time. Tell a child you're taking him or her to the circus on Saturday at 2 p.m., and the child will not just take you at your word; he or she will actually start planning what circus acts they're going to see, how much cotton candy they'll eat, which friends they'll tell afterwards! The car could break down on Friday night—*not a problem!* You, the parent, could be told you have to work on Saturday—*doesn't matter!* The circus could move on to the next town—*so what?!* YOU made a PROMISE, and the child has just as much faith in your promise as he or she has in the sun rising the next morning. Nothing can prevent it. IT'S A REALITY!

That's how God wants us to treat all the promises in the Bible. Even if we can't see any progress being made, even if things "appear" to be going south, He wants us to consider His Word a done deal. A supernatural reality more real than our current circumstances and present prospects. That's FAITH! That's CHILD-LIKE faith—the kind Christ desires for us! (Matthew 18:3)

"...Without faith it is impossible to please God, because anyone who comes to him must believe that he exists and that he rewards those who earnestly seek him." (Hebrews 11:6 NIV)

Rocky Road to Success

During his birth, in July 1946, a mishandled forceps delivery severed a nerve on the lower left side of Sylvester Stallone's face, causing partial paralysis of his lip, tongue, and chin. As a result, Stallone grew up with slightly slurred speech and a sad, drowsy-eyed countenance. In school the other kids taunted him. At age nine his parents divorced, and for a time, Stallone was shuttled from one foster home to another. But the talented American actor, director and screenwriter didn't let any of these circumstances hold him back in life. His disadvantaged childhood was only the first round in a grueling fight to be a success.

Early in his acting career Stallone struggled to support himself. He took bit parts in television shows and cheap films, but it was never enough. He was evicted from his apartment and ended up sleeping in a New York City Bus Terminal for three weeks. Stallone once said, "...I was at the end—the very end—of my rope." At one particularly low point, in order to keep his electricity turned on, the actor was forced to sell his best friend, a Bullmastiff named Butkus, for $25.

About two weeks later, early in 1975, Stallone saw the Muhammad Ali and Chuck Wepner heavyweight boxing match. That night Stallone went home and started writing the script for the movie *Rocky*. Three days later, and after 20 straight hours of writing, he'd completed it. Then started the next grueling round, actually several rounds: he tried repeatedly to sell his script, and repeatedly it was rejected. In fact, Stallone received hundreds of *NO!*s Maybe one deterrent was his stipulation that whichever studio purchased the script also had to hire him to play the title role. The actor knew his concept was a valuable property, and he also knew he was born to play Rocky Balboa. It was his best shot, his chance of a lifetime, and he refused to throw in the towel.

Finally, United Artists offered to buy the script for $125,000. But the studio wanted a big star for the lead role, perhaps Robert Redford or Burt Reynolds. Stallone was actually the LAST person UA wanted for the part. The studio didn't think he could act and that he wouldn't be believable in the role of a weary club fighter who suddenly gets a shot at the World Heavyweight title. So Stallone refused their offer.

But producers Irwin Winkler and Robert Chartoff really wanted Stallone's script. They upped their offer to $350,000, but they were adamant that someone else would play Rocky. Oh yeah? Bottom line, UA got the script and Stallone got the part, a plum role for a virtu-ally unknown actor. But the studio had grave doubts the movie would succeed without a more talented, better-known performer, so they drastically cut the film's production budget and agreed to pay Stallone a paltry $35,000 plus a percentage of the profits—should the movie make any!

Stallone immediately used the money to buy back his dog—for a whopping $15,000—proving that: a) some opportunistic person took advantage of the actor's wind-fall; b) Stallone really loved that pooch; and c) dogs may be the world's greatest financial investment!

Rocky was made for $1,000,000; pretty cheap even for 1976. The movie proved both a critical and popular success. It won the Oscar for Best Picture, and grossed over $200 million. Not bad. And Stallone, the down and out actor, an unknown quantity who kept slugging it out for what he believed in, received two Academy Award nominations that year: for Best Actor and Best Dramatic Screenplay. Stallone went the distance with his dream. The actor can say, just as his Rocky character shouts it from the ring at the movie's end: "I did it!"

Don't give up! And if you have deep convictions about a project, then don't give in! "Keep standing firm in your faith. Keep on being courageous and strong." (1 Corinthians 16:13 ISV)

"I can do all things through Christ who strengthens me."
(Philippians 4:13 Jubilee Bible 2000)

SETBACK OR COMEBACK?

How we face failure can determine our future success. If you're a creator and you accept rejection or defeat as the end of the line, you're not going to get very far in life. We can view failure either as an impassible roadblock, or simply as a detour.

No one ever plans to take a detour, but sometimes a detour can put us on a different track that leads to better places and bigger opportunities. Mistakes and false starts aren't necessarily the worst thing that can happen to us. Losing heart and throwing in the towel IS! T.D. Jakes once said, "A setback is a setup for a comeback!" This is certainly true in the case of a draftsman named Milton Bradley.

Bradley was born in Maine on November 8, 1836, and grew up in a working-class household in Massachusetts. After completing high school in 1854, Bradley quickly found work as a draftsman and patent agent. Once he'd earned the tuition fees, he enrolled in the Lawrence Scientific School in Cambridge.

In 1856, Bradley got a job with Blanchard & Kimball's locomotive works in Springfield, Massachusetts. A nice steady job with a good future—or so he thought. During the economic recession of 1858, the company offices closed, and Bradley suddenly found his career opportunities extremely limited. So he followed the example of other enterprising young men who couldn't get a job: he entered business for himself—doing what he knew best, working as a mechanical draftsman and patent agent.

But there was still a recession! In 1859, Bradley went to Providence, RI to learn lithography. Armed with yet another skill, he set up a color lithography shop the following year, in Springfield. It was the first of its kind in the city, a business that just had to succeed. Or *not.* Bradley was about to encounter his greatest setback, and suffer a financial blow that might have signaled the end of his entrepreneurial career.

Springfield was the stomping ground—*er, stumping ground?*—of a little-known Republican who was about to run for president of the United States. Bradley decided to print and sell color lithographs of the presidential nominee, and the venture proved quite successful—initially. The prints were selling like hotcakes until the man depicted in Bradley's lithographs did something that completely changed his appearance. The guy grew a thick and distinctively shaped beard. Suddenly, Bradley's not-so-loyal customers were demanding their money back, arguing that the lithograph was no longer an accurate depiction of the man they all hoped would be their next Commander-in-Chief—Abraham Lincoln! Realizing the prints were now essentially worthless, Bradley burned his remaining stock.

While sitting in his office, trying to figure out how he could possibly recoup this financial loss, poor Bradley decided to give his fevered brain a little break, by playing a board game a friend had given him. Playing the game and contemplating the ups and downs of life, business and success, Milton Bradley suddenly got the idea that would forever change his fortunes and jumpstart a business that prospers to this day!

The draftsman-turned-patent agent, turned-lithographer created the Checkered Game of Life. He released his new board game shortly before Christmas in 1860. Its sales were AMAZING!

Today, people are still playing The Game of Life, along with other Milton Bradley Company games such as Operation and Battleship. All because a hard working entrepreneur chose to view a financial setback as an opportunity for a creative comeback!

"...The LORD your God turned the curse into a blessing for you, because the LORD your God loved you." (Deuteronomy 23:5 ESV)

DOWN BUT NOT OUT!

Failures, repeated failures, are the finger posts on the road to achievement. One fails forward toward success.
—C.S. Lewis

Ever get knocked down? Of course you have. Life sometimes has a way of blindsiding us. We get knocked off our feet by adversity, but sometimes we just trip over our own shortcomings. Sooner or later we all stumble and fall short of the mark. When we do, it's important we rise again, shake off the dust of disappointment, and move on with our lives.

Failure and adversity can become roadblocks to personal, artistic, and financial success. They can make you drop your pen, put down your brush, stop typing, stop playing, stop performing, maybe even stop living. Or we can view failure and adversity as just potholes in the road of life. We get jolted by them, temporarily knocked off course, and we may even need to stop a moment to effect some repairs; but then we get moving again.

There's a great actor who faced his share of adversity while growing up. His father was a drug addict who expressed his love in the only way he knew, by passing a joint to his six-year-old son. We'd like to say the boy quickly overcame this adversity, but he didn't. Like his father he became an addict. But it's not how we *begin*, but how we *end* that's important. And sometimes, the greatest heights are achieved after hitting rock-bottom.

After years of substance abuse, Robert Downey, Jr. hit bottom. A series of arrests on drug-related charges, court dates, rehab and relapse, culminated in six months spent in jail. But afterwards, Downey was ready to get his act together. "It's not that difficult to overcome these seemingly ghastly problems," he once stated. "What's hard is to decide to do it."

After overcoming this failure in life, the actor then faced more adversity, more potholes. Both Downey's history with drugs and his reputation for being less than dependable were well known in the film industry. Few directors were willing to take a chance on him, and those who were, had difficulty getting the actor insured. Downey needed to prove himself all over again, and the actor who'd been nominated for an Oscar, for portraying Charlie Chaplin, now found himself playing supporting parts in television and minor film productions. His substance abuse had cost him a major setback.

T.D. Jakes often states, "A setback is a setup for a comeback," and Downey worked hard to come back.

Ironically, during more than two decades of acting, he'd never appeared in a blockbuster movie. And after all he'd been through, it was hard to think he ever would. But in 2008, director Jon Favreau wanted Downey for the title role of *Iron Man*. A lot of very nervous executives must have said "No way!" Besides, comic book heroes are drawn larger than life: young, muscled and at least 6 feet tall. Downey is 5' 8" and, at the time, was 43 and slender. But you can't keep a good actor *down-ey*. (Ouch, we promise not to do that again.)

Favreau insisted, and the nervous executives gave in. Then Downey bulked up and stood on his giant talent. The rest is box-office history. All of the Iron Man movies have been phenomenally successful, and today Downey is the highest paid actor in Hollywood. Not a bad comeback.

Have you suffered some setbacks? Ready for a comeback? Just remember, "Success is not final, failure is not fatal: it is the courage to continue that counts." (Winston Churchill)

You may be *down-ey* for the count, but you're not out! (*Heh*, we did it again!)

THE CURIOUS CASE OF THE NEGLECTED NOVEL

She loved apples, playing the piano, and a good game of golf. Mostly, however, she loved writing. She wrote in the bathtub, on the washstand, at the dining room table—and when she spent time in the Middle East, she wrote on a makeshift table of boards and packing crates. For decades she averaged two novels a year, writing them longhand at first, but eventually using a typewriter.

She's the greatest mystery writer of all time, producing 78 detective novels, over 100 short stories, and 19 plays, including *Mousetrap*—the world's longest-running play, which opened in London's West End in 1952 and is still running today after more than 25,000 performances. Most of her books and short stories have been adapted for television and feature films. According to the *Guinness Book of World Records*, she's the best-selling novelist of all time. Her work has been translated in over a hundred languages, making her the single most-translated author; and her books have sold over two billion copies. Only the Bible and Shakespeare have outsold her.

All these accomplishments because Agatha Christie persevered. She refused to take "no" for an answer.

Dame Agatha Christie was born in 1890, in the Devon coast town of Torquay. She grew up with a passion for detective novels. She devoured the Sherlock Holmes stories of Sir Arthur Conan Doyle, and such novels as Wilkie Collins' *The Woman in White* and *The Moonstone*. One day, Agatha's sister challenged her to write a mystery novel of her own. Agatha produced her first detective novel, *The Mysterious Affair at Styles*.

Over the next four years Agatha tried repeatedly to find a home for her book. Not one publisher took even the slightest interest in her manuscript. One account states the author received close to 500 rejections during this time. The mystery novelist was about to forever change the rules of detective fiction—it's just that no one realized it at the time.

In 1920, the publishing company Bodley Head showed genuine interest in Agatha's novel. The editor John Lane eventually offered the young writer a contract, after procrastinating for close to a year. He asked Agatha to change the ending—which she promptly did— and then paid her a mere £25. So, five years after Agatha finished *The Mysterious Affair at Styles*, the novel that launched the career of the brilliant Belgian detective Hercule Poirot finally saw print.

Agatha Christie was on her way. A few years later she published *And Then There Were None*, also known as *Ten Little Indians*, and the basis for several movies and TV shows. To date, the book has sold over 100 million copies, making it the world's best-selling mystery—ever!

Don't stop at "No"! Keep trying. Rejection is one of life's great mysteries. We may not always understand it, but we all have to endure it.

"Trust in the Lord and do good.... Take delight in the Lord, and he will give you the desires of your heart. Commit your way to the Lord; trust in him and he will do this.... Be still before the Lord and wait patiently for him...." (Psalm 37:3-7 NIV)

Don't Let a Smile

Become a Frown!

Each year, thousands of designers, artists, inventors and businesspeople come up with multi-million dollar ideas. Some of these men and women instantly recognize the potential of their creations, and cry EUREKA! Others apparently don't realize what they have. They view their creations as "throwaway ideas"; serving only an immediate need; perfect for the moment, not much else. They minimize their own dreams and creativity, believing their creations are not that innovative, not that extraordinary, not that much of a big deal. Humility? Or shortsightedness? Often they fail to see the full potential of their inventiveness, or its possible future applications—a bitter lesson Harvey Ross Ball probably knew well.

Ball was an American graphic artist and advertising man. In 1963, one of Ball's clients, State Mutual Life Assurance Company, commissioned Ball to come up with a simple cartoon design, which they planned to distribute throughout the company on memos and buttons. The insurance company had just gone through a complex and stressful restructuring, and they hoped the design would help boost the morale of their employees. Ball quickly sketched a yellow circle with two crooked eyes and a winsome smile—the prototype of what eventually became the Smiley Face. It took the artist a mere ten minutes to come up with the idea and dash it off. He was paid $45 for his labor and, at the time, probably felt well compensated for what's essentially a doodle. The insurance company plastered Ball's smiley design on posters, signs and thousands of buttons. Soon, other businesses were copying it.

But no big deal. Neither Ball nor State Mutual bothered to trademark the image. After all, how could they know the little yellow face with the big smile would become so popular, even fifty years later, or that the smiley would make someone (NOT them) filthy rich?

In 1971, a French newspaper publisher, Franklin Loufrani, decided to use a variation of Ball's design in the logo of his paper, to remind readers that not all news is bad. And it's Loufrani who named the little guy Smiley. You must surely know the rest of this story— the smiley is profitably marketed throughout the world today—but it's possible there's one little detail you don't know: since neither Harvey Ball nor State Mutual bothered to register their creation, Loufrani decided to trademark both the design and the name "Smiley" in 1988. Loufrani launched the Smiley Company and began selling tee-shirts, but in 1996 his son Nicolas took over the family business and transformed it into one of the top 100 licensing companies in the world.

Today, the Smiley Company makes over $130 million a year. One of its most significant licensing agreements was for all those tiny emoticons we use when texting on our phones and tablets. But good old Smiley shows up everywhere—stickers, mugs, hats, greeting cards, you name it!—making it the most recognizable icon in the world, with a smile second only to that of the Mona Lisa. Not bad for a 10-minute, $45 doodle.

Lesson: little ideas can be like little stones thrown into a pond, and make big ripples in life. Small beginnings can lead to bigger and better things. And no goal is insignificant. Never underestimate a good concept, and believe in your own dreams. Above all, have faith in God and in the creativity with which He's gifted you. And Have A Nice Day! ☺

"Do not despise these small beginnings, for the LORD rejoices to see the work begin...." (Zechariah 4:10 NLT)

SENDING OUT AN S.O.S.

Ever feel like you've lost your vision? Like you're swamped with the problems of life, and your dreams are slowly sinking, drowning in a sea of "stuff"? If your unfulfilled goals could talk, would they cry for help? Would your neglected dreams, feeling as though the end might be near, send out a distress signal—an S.O.S.?

In the case of goals, dreams, and visions, that S.O.S. is a plea for very specific action. If we're to find the time, energy and resources necessary to pursue our goals and rescue our unfulfilled dreams, then we need to do three things. Quickly, before it's too late.

Part I: The *first* letter of our S.O.S. for Dreamers stands for *SIMPLIFY!* It's absolutely the first course of action in any rescue operation. If your life is too complicated you'll be mostly ineffective at accomplishing the things necessary to keep you moving forward in the pursuit of your goals. Your time, energy, and resources are limited, so it's imperative to wisely manage these assets. Simplifying your life is the best way to start. We suggest several key areas of life that tend to get "tangled up": areas where there's too much, activities that are too often, things that are too complicated.

1. Simplify your schedule: chances are, you have too many activities planned for too little time. Come on, do you really think you can do everything? You can only accomplish so much in a day, a year, a life. Decide what's most important—like achieving your goals—and limit your other activities. No, don't become obsessed, but realize your time and energy are precious, and simplify these other areas:

2. Simplify your recreations: sports, hobbies, TV, video games, interests, etc. If you go jogging every day, followed by a few rounds of golf or a game of tennis with a friend, you'll have far less time and energy to accomplish your goals. Leisure time and light distractions are good for our mental health, and hobbies are fun, but we need to limit how many pastimes we have and how often we indulge in them, if we intend to get anything else done. For instance, TV and theatrical movies are entertaining, but trying to keep up with over a dozen weekly shows and take in every new movie could be the death of your dreams. *S.O.S!*

3. Simplify your Finances: Remember, every time a department store sales clerk talks you into opening a charge account with them, you are further complicating your finances and your life. Getting 10% off your first purchase is tempting, but you'll pay for it later. We know people with dozens and dozens of store cards, and they spend hours and hours keeping track of their purchases and making sure each account gets paid on time. Who needs the headache? Similarly, we know people who belong to dozens of book clubs, movie clubs, etc., and they're drowning in those crazy little cards demanding they reply by a certain date. *S.O.S!*

4. Simplify your Relationships: This may sound sacrilegious, but you can have too many "friends"! All meaningful relationships require time, energy and commitment. "A friend in need is a friend indeed," so lots of friends eventually equate to lots of needs. Friends need time to get together, socialize, catch up, vent. S.O.S! How many hours are there in a week—AFTER you subtract work and family responsibilities? Limit your friends to a few and you'll also reduce your number of social obligations. Now, this doesn't mean you stop being friendly! Jesus is our example. When He walked the earth He was friendly to everyone. But He had only a handful of close friends.

5. Simplify your Purpose and Focus: Decide what you'd like to accomplish in life. Pick a couple goals and narrow your focus. Master a few things, instead of being mediocre in many things. Again, Jesus is our example. He healed the sick, fed the multitudes, and taught the masses; but Jesus never lost sight of His primary mission: the Cross! Which is why He limited all the other activities and ministries that could have kept Him too busy. (John 6:5) *S.O.S!*

Are your leisure-time "distractions" distracting you a little too much? Are you tied up in paperwork and payment deadlines from overly complicated finances? Do too many friends keep you busy chatting and texting and meeting for lunch? Do you feel pulled in several directions at once? *S.O.S.!*

Simplify! "...Martha was distracted with all her prep-arations; ...But the Lord...said to her, 'Martha, Martha, you are worried and bothered about so many things; but only one thing is necessary....'" (Luke 10:40-42 NASB)

THE "OHH!" IN S.O.S.
(PART II)

Let all things be done decently and in order.
—1 Corinthians 14: 40 KJV

Are your dreams shipwrecked on an island of neglect? Are your goals drowning in a sea of too many activities, interests and responsibilities? If your unfulfilled dreams could talk, would they be sending out an S.O.S.!?

If you want to find the time, energy and resources necessary to pursue your goals and rescue your dreams, then you probably need to take three important steps. The first step is to simplify key areas of your life: your schedule, finances, hobbies and interests, as well as your relationships and your focus. Too much "stuff," too many "friends," too many interests, too many direc-tions—can leave you confused and dazed, with no time or energy for your dreams. So, the first letter in S.O.S. stands for *simplify*.

Part 2: *The "O" stands for ORGANIZE!* Everything! Your home, your kitchen, your office, your desk or creative space. Believe it or not, clutter can impede the ability to think clearly. And from a practical standpoint, you can accomplish more in less time, IF you're not continually shuffling through drawers, files, stacks of papers; looking for whatever it is you need in order to get something done. Think about a cook in a disorganized kitchen, where the drawers are a jumbled mess and dishes are piled on the counter. While trying to prepare a meal, the poor cook will be digging for the right utensils, pushing pots out of the way to free up work space, and running back and forth while accomplishing very little. But your organization shouldn't be confined to physical spaces.

Organize your finances. You'll spend less time wondering which bills are due when, and whether or not you've already paid them. Result: less stress, no surprises, more time and energy to pursue goals. "...God is not the author of confusion, but of peace...." (1 Corinthians 14: 33 KJV)

Organize your schedule. Know what needs to be done—and when—and prioritize your responsibilities. Keep notes and make lists, to help remind you of things you need, projects you should be working on, pressing responsibilities and deadlines. If you're driving into town, make it count, by arranging and scheduling other things you can accomplish on your trip. The last thing you want is to waste time. And if you suddenly find yourself waiting, seemingly with nothing to do, you can pull out your "Things to Do" list. Chances are you have calls to make, a bill you can pay on your phone, etc.—or you can spend the time updating your list!

Organize your free time. Yes, there are occasions when it's nice to hide the clocks, find a spot of ocean sand, throw down a blanket, and just listen to the surf. But if you do this too often, we doubt you'll fulfill your dreams. People will remember you as a beach bum and not as someone who achieved great goals. Balance is key: realize how much of your time will be spent playing video games versus pursuing your dreams.

Organize! Some people know well in advance what needs to be done, how long it will take, how to go about doing it, and when to start. They're organized, and hence more efficient: they get more done in less time. Other people run about squawking like chickens with no heads —and they accomplish very little!

"Don't live like fools, but like those who are wise. Make the most of every opportunity...."

(Ephesians 5: 15-16 NLT)

THE LAST LETTER OF S.O.S.
(PART III)

Are your aspirations drowning in a sea of too many activities, interests and responsibilities? If your unfulfilled goals and neglected dreams could talk, would they be sending out an S.O.S.? We've been discussing the steps necessary to rescue "shipwrecked" dreams. The first step (the first letter in *S.O.S.*) is to simplify key areas of your life: your schedule, finances, hobbies and interests, as well as your relationships and your focus. Too much "stuff," too many "friends," too many interests, too many directions, can leave you confused and dazed, with no time or energy for your goals.

The second step (the "O" in *S.O.S.*) is to organize—*everything!* Your home, kitchen, office, desk, or creative space. Clutter impedes creativity and the ability to think clearly. Organize your finances, your schedule, and your free time. Know what needs to be done—and when—and prioritize your responsibilities.

Part 3: *The last "S" in S.O.S. stands for Strategize!* Face it, it's not enough simply to set goals. Dreams usually don't come true all by their lonesome. We have to constantly pursue them or they tend to get away. We have to map out what we want to accomplish in life, and then strategize how we'll go about doing it. We need a plan of attack—a battle plan, so to speak! Being victorious in life is like being victorious in a war. Great wars are won with smaller victories won in battles. Your goals will be achieved in much the same way, through the small victories and accomplishments that move you closer to winning your bigger dreams.

Achieving any truly great dream is much like waging a war: to overcome the obstacles imposed by time, resources, circumstances, and even people who don't want to see you succeed (for various reasons). Are you strategizing to win the small battles you encounter each day? Every day you should map out what you need to accomplish and what it will take to do it. Create a schedule. Maintain a list of "Things to do." Prioritize your list. Work to achieve something worthwhile every day. Even little steps, when carefully planned each day, can take you far along the path to success.

Do you need special training to accomplish your goals? Do you need capital? Do you need a staff? Figure out what your requirements are and how you'll go about meeting them. Strategize your short term goals, and decide how each piece fits into the bigger picture. Stay focused and use your time wisely. Stay on the right track and keep moving forward.

In other words, stop flying by the seat of your pants; you gotta have a plan! Even God had a plan—a *loooong*-term plan, with many intricate and interlocking elements and events:

"...God saved us and called us to live a holy life. He did this, not because we deserved it, but because that was his plan from before the beginning of time—to show us his grace through Christ Jesus." (2 Timothy 1: 9 NLT)

THE IMPOSSIBLE DREAM!

Listen to this message from the LORD, you nations of the world; proclaim it in distant coastlands: The LORD, who scattered his people, will gather them and watch over them as a shepherd does his flock.

—Jeremiah 31:10 NLT

A dream of redemption, of rebuilding, of returning HOME:

Modern Israel, roughly located on the lands of the ancient kingdoms of Israel and Judah, is tiny—about the size of Wales or New Jersey. It's the birthplace of the Hebrew language and of Judaism and Christianity. Although the region welcomed a variety of ethnicities, and weathered the influence and interference of several empires, the region remained predominantly Jewish until the 3rd century. Afterwards, the Israeli people endured hundreds of years of religious and cultural persecution that led them to flee their homeland, scattering throughout the world—where they remained as strangers in strange lands, further persecuted and forever alienated.

Many Jews dreamed of a place they could call their own...a home, a haven. But after centuries of being harassed, uprooted, dispersed—and even murdered— their dream seemed like an impossible one.

Theodor Herzl shared their "impossible dream." He was an Austro-Hungarian journalist, political activist, and writer. More importantly, he became one of the fathers of modern Zionism, forming the World Zionist Organization and promoting Jewish migration back to the region renamed Palestine, in an effort to recreate the Jewish nation of Israel. Herzl (May 2, 1860-July 3, 1904) was born in Budapest, Hungary, to a family of secular, German-speaking, assimilated Jews. His father was a successful German businessman who tried to blend in.

Theodor Herzl, was not a religious man. He had a passion for poetry and the humanities, which led to a successful career in journalism. But despite having no religious affiliation with Jews, despite being a successful writer, and the son of a successful businessman, despite being assimilated (blending in), Herzl nonetheless felt the sting of anti-Semitism. Bottom line? Herzl was a Jew.

Herzl believed that anti-Semitism could not be defeated or cured, only avoided. In his acclaimed 1896 book *The Jewish State*, he outlined reasons for Jews to leave Europe, should they desire, preferably to return to their historic homeland. Herzl believed the Jewish people already possessed a nationality and all they lacked was a nation. He fervently believed the only way to avoid anti-Semitism was for the Jewish people to have their own state, where they'd be free to practice their unique culture and religion. Little could Herzl imagine the greatest time of persecution, the Holocaust, was only four decades away—less than a lifetime; and if the modern State of Israel had been established prior to the Holocaust, the massacre of 6 million Jews could have been avoided.

Herzl's ideas quickly spread and, although embraced by many, were largely criticized and rejected—

ironically, by many Jews settled in many countries. These critical Jews, who at the time were attempting to blend in and gain acceptance by the gentile population, felt Herzl's ideas would only fan the flames of anti-Semitism. But think about it: should any person or people group have to deny their origins, beliefs, culture, identity, and individuality to gain acceptance? What's our message? ACCEPTANCE.

Undeterred by his detractors, Herzl enthusiastically pursued his impossible dream. He gained influential and powerful supporters in several countries, and with each passing year, his impossible dream advanced into the realm of the possible. Although Herzl wouldn't see it realized before his death, his work had laid the foundation to make his dream a reality.

On November 29, 1947, the United Nations recommended a new Jewish state. On May 15, 1948, David Ben-Gurion, who became Israel's first Prime Minister, declared "the establishment of a Jewish state...to be known as the State of Israel"! On the same day, the United States, in the person of President Harry Truman, officially recognized the new Jewish nation.

Today, more than 42% of the world's Jews reside in the State of Israel, making it the largest Jewish community in the world. Israel is their home, their freedom, and their vindication. May 15, 2015 was the nation's 67th Birthday, a time of celebration and thanksgiving...a time to acknowledge that dreams, even impossible ones, can come true!

He's Still the Man!

We last wrote of how the dream of the Jews ever returning to their homeland and establishing a Jewish nation,
seemed an impossible one. But even "impossible"
dreams can come true! Such is the case of a writer and
creator who typifies the indomitable spirit of the impossible dreamer, a guy named Stanley Martin Lieber,
whose aspiration was to pen the Great American Novel.
But the road to fulfilling one's destiny can be long and
meandering. It might even hold a surprising detour or
two. Stanley never wrote anything quite as revered as
Melville's *Moby Dick* or Hawthorne's *The Scarlet Letter*,
but he did manage to... *well*, we're getting ahead of ourselves. First things first.

The oldest of two sons, Stanley was born to Roma-
nian Jewish immigrants, in Manhattan, New York on
December 28, 1922. During his teens, Stanley's family
weathered the Great Depression, eventually downsizing
to a one-bedroom apartment in the Bronx, where he
shared the bedroom with his brother, Larry. The boys'
parents slept on a foldout couch.

After attending high school in the Bronx, Lee began
his journey to becoming a Great American Author...by
delivering sandwiches for a local pharmacy to offices in
Rockefeller Center, by ushering at the Rivoli Theater on
Broadway, and by selling subscriptions to the *New York*

Herald Tribune. Oh, and he also worked as an office boy for a company that made men's pants. Lee did, however, get occasional writing jobs: mostly composing obituaries for a news service.

In 1939, with a little help from an uncle, Stanley found a position as an "assistant" at the newly-formed Timely Comics. The publisher of Timely, Martin Goodman, was the husband of Stanley's cousin Jean— so no one could quite label this as an act of nepotism. Initially, Stanley filled inkwells and fetched lunches for the staff, which included Joe Simon and Jack Kirby, two Jewish guys who'd just created Captain America! Later, the young writer graduated to proofreading and even got to pen a one-page Captain America filler. When he wrote his first comic book material, he did so under a pseudonym. Stanley was saving his real name for literary fame.

Stanley soon found himself writing full-length comics stories; and in 1941, when Simon and Kirby abruptly left the company following a dispute with the publisher, Goodman promoted the 19-year-old "assistant" to interim editor. But Stanley demonstrated such a talent for the business that Goodman eventually made him editor-in-chief, a position Stanley held until 1972, when he actually succeeded Goodman as publisher.

Along the way, as he traveled further and *farther* down the road to his destiny, Stanley watched his dream of writing the Great American novel fade in the distance. He was kept too busy writing the tales of "superheroes" for four-color comic books, a not very respectable, "toss-away" medium. Whenever friends asked him exactly what he wrote, Stanley would hesitantly tell them he wrote "children's literature." But he kept his chin up and made the most of his opportunities. For instance, when the popularity of superheroes waned during the 1950s, Stanley created and wrote a string of wildly popular horror comics, along with romance and western features—whatever was selling at the time.

By the 1960s, there was a resurgence of interest in superheroes. Over at DC Comics, home of Superman and Batman, many of the company's previously moth-balled characters were being rebooted. And Goodman took particular notice that DC was enjoying great success by teaming up several of its heroes in a single comics magazine. So he asked Stanley to create a team-up comic for his own "MCG" line of comics. Well, by now Stanley was feeling trapped in a fast lane leading him far away from the novel he longed to write. Partly as an escape, partly because his wife encouraged him to take creative liberties, Stanley wrote a story about a some-what dysfunctional team of reluctant heroes for a comic book that was years ahead of its time; he created *The Fantastic Four.*

Stanley Martin Leiber, the kid who wrote under the name of Stan Lee because he didn't want to be asso-ciated with comic books, never did write that novel. But Stan "the Man" Lee did go on to create or co-create dozens more characters, including Iron Man, the Hulk, and Thor, and he also successfully rebooted Captain America—"literary" characters that became household names and spawned a multi-billion dollar industry; intellectual properties that continue to provide the inspiration for Hollywood's biggest box-office hits.

Today, at age 92, Stan Lee is still happily working with comic book characters; and after 67 years of wedded bliss, his wife, actress Joan B Lee, proudly proclaims that Stan is still "the Man." He continues to guide the characters he created, as an executive producer for each new movie in Disney's tremendously successful Marvel Cinematic Universe; and in every one of these movies, he can be seen in a brief cameo role, hamming it up, having a blast, embracing his destiny—

and enjoying his status as one of the greatest, most famous writers of fiction the world has known.

As Stan Lee might add, "'Nuff said, True Believers!"

LOVE & THE REJECTED PILOT

Sometimes a creator can have a great idea or produce a masterpiece, but still encounter rejection. Perhaps the timing isn't right, or the wrong people are considering the material or, as in the case we're about to share, the right people are considering the work but they just don't get it or are too blind to see its merits. This is often true of television production. In fact, when it comes to programming for television, there's often a good reason the TV is called the boob tube, and no, it's not a reference to the viewers.

In 1970, successful comedy writer/producer Garry Marshall had a great idea for a new television series—at least, that's what he thought at the time—about life and love in an innocent bygone time. Miller-Milkis Productions filmed a pilot for the new show, calling it *New Family in Town*. The parent studio, Paramount Pictures was unimpressed, and the ABC network passed on the idea. No one at the time thought Garry Marshall would be able to sustain a comedy series so immersed in nostalgia for more than a season or two, at best; and besides, the decision-makers at ABC didn't particularly care for the young man Miller-Milkis had cast as the lead. The idea for a series was shelved, and the network "burned off" the pilot episode as an installment of its anthology show *Love, American Style*, retitling the segment, somewhat ironically, "Love and the Television Set"! (Remember all those anthology shows that proliferated the airwaves from about 1954 through the early '80s? Well, think *Twilight Zone*; except that during the last couple minutes of each episode of *Love, American Style*, instead of one of Rod Serling's shocking twist endings, there's just a lot of smooching and blushing.)

A year later, a pre-*Star Wars* George Lucas was casting *American Graffiti*, his humorous, uber-nostalgic film based on his experiences with fast cars and adolescence circa 1962. Lucas viewed Marshall's unsold pilot and immediately decided to cast its star (what's-his-name, the guy the ABC executives weren't particularly impressed with) in the lead role of his new movie. When released in 1973, *American Graffiti* became an instant classic and proved itself to be box office gold! (So the actor, what's-his-name, was vindicated. But that's not our point here, nor is it the end of our story.)

Over at ABC, the suits were salivating. Legend has it that one of them remarked to an underling that the network should come up with a new nostalgic comedy to capitalize on the success of *American Graffiti*. "Run out and get someone to create a pilot," he snapped.

The underling carefully told his boss that the network already had a pilot for just such a series: "And it even stars what's-his-name from the movie!"

"Why haven't I seen it, then?" barked his boss.

"But you did, your greatness! [Okay, yes, we're exaggerating here...a little.] Don't you remember? You shelved the project!"

We're not sure if the poor underling kept his job, but ABC hurried the series into production, and a few months later, the ABC comedy *Happy Days*, starring

Ron Howard, premiered in January 1974. The show was an immediate success and creator Garry Marshall kept people laughing through 11 seasons. So much for being able to sustain a show about love set in the 1950s! Throughout the rest of the '70s, the show was consistently ranked among the top 20 most-watched shows. Yes, it's a silly sitcom, but if you were growing up around that time, you probably know how popular and influential it was. ABC spun off seven other series from *Happy Days*, two of which were also ratings successes. There also were books, comics, toys, and lunch boxes. (Now, doesn't *every* creator want to see his or her stuff plastered on a kid's lunch box?!) And lest we forget, *Happy Days* is responsible for a few well-known idioms, such as "jumped the shark"!

Moral of the above anecdote: often, rejection is far from being the end of a creator's journey! Wrong time, wrong place, wrong response; consider such things as just speed bumps on the road to success!

IT'S ABOUT TIME!

In 1965, American writer Harlan Ellison published the multiple award-winning short story "'Repent, Harlequin!' Said the Ticktockman"; a dystopian fantasy depicting a world in which the machinery of civilization is rigidly governed by the clock, by strict adherence to schedules and an unerring observation of deadlines. In Ellison's cautionary tale, time has become so precious that to waste even a minute of it is punishable by having an equal amount of time subtracted from one's lifespan, via the programmed cardioplate given each citizen. Into this crazy world comes the masked hero popularly known as the Harlequin. His mission: to disrupt schedules, to disregard deadlines, to be...late! (Sound like anyone you know?)

Ellison once acknowledged that he's notorious for being late, and here the writer is no doubt enjoying the opportunity to respond to his critics. In his story, however, the actions of our hero have come under the scrutiny of a terrifying government agency that holds over the citizenry the power of life and death—*no, not the IRS*—the office of the dreaded Master Timekeeper! Feared by all, and infamously nicknamed the Ticktockman, the Master Timekeeper estimates that the Harlequin has cost the people so much time, that he has completely exhausted his own quota of minutes, days, years. So the Ticktockman vows that if he ever learns the secret identity of the masked man, he will terminate his cardioplate.

In a world where time is the single most precious commodity, the Harlequin is bankrupt! Our poor hero truly has run out of time! So then what happens? Ellison's tale is allegedly one of the ten most reprinted stories in the English language. You should have no difficulty finding and reading it. It's a fun piece of roller-coaster prose, and we mention it not because we're advocates of habitual tardiness: showing up fashionably late for every occasion may look cool, but it's a bad habit that can easily backfire; and although tardy people never take time to analyze their actions, they are ultimately showing a disregard for the rights and feelings of those they inconvenience. No one likes to be kept waiting. (*Uhm*, please consider this a special public service message. We now resume our regularly scheduled article, already in progress.)

What we'd like to share with dreamers today is that TIME IS A COMMODITY. We never want to reach the point where we're obsessed with it or bound by it; but since each of us is allotted just 24 hours a day to accomplish multiple tasks, we need to spend our time wisely. If we're actively pursuing a dream, trying to reach a goal, then we'll always have important things to do, places to go, people to see. So, we can't afford to squander our time on unproductive activities that don't add value to our physical, emotional or spiritual well-being—and which don't get us any closer to our goals.

Okay, let's clarify something: we periodically take time to go for a walk, play a board game, or watch a good movie. We need such diversions to help keep our sanity. But maintaining a balance is essential. And if you have unfulfilled dreams, you need to stay focused. Ben Franklin once said, "Time is money." Not exactly true, but close enough. Time is a valuable resource you can't replenish. When it's gone...it's gone! If you view time the same way you should be viewing money, then you'll have a better grasp of how important time is, and how to maintain the proper balance. Example: You get paid (you have some time on your hands), but how will you spend your resources? You first need to take care of some nagging debts (social obligations); then you decide to invest for your future (devote time to achieving your dreams); finally, you have something leftover and you decide to spring for a mocha latte and a Cinnabon (you spend some leisure time doing something absolutely mindless, if you want, like playing tiddlywinks).

Don't be obsessed, but never lose sight of the bigger picture. Spend your time wisely. Remember, the next time you're goofing off (excessively so), that instead, you could be hatching grand schemes and chasing big dreams! (It's our favorite sport!)

Next we'll examine the flip-side of this issue, and discuss the importance of being a Time Lord, not a Time Hoard! Please don't be late, friends!

"...Walk, not as unwise but as wise, making the best use of the time, because the days are evil." (1 Corinthians 5:15-16 ESV)

Time Lord or Time Hoard?

Time keeps on slippin', slippin', slippin'; into the future!
—Steve Miller, "Fly Like an Eagle"

We previously mentioned that time is our most valuable commodity. We're granted a certain amount of it, and when it's gone it's gone! So we need to use it wisely. But time, like money, is also a precious resource that needs to be shared. If we're pursuing a dream, working to achieve a goal, we tend to be stingy with our time. We tend to use our resources, including time, sparingly. It's easy to get the mindset that we can't afford to spend any of our precious time for anything or anyone but ourselves. Like a miser, we begin to hoard our time. But do we really want to get that obsessed with our dreams? Is that truly the ticket to success?

"Successful people are always looking for opportunities to help others. Unsuccessful people are always asking, 'What's in it for me?'" (Brian Taylor, Author and Speaker on Self Development)

But what does God think? "Give, and you will receive. Your gift will return to you in full—pressed down, shaken together to make room for more, running over, and poured into your lap. The amount you give will determine the amount you get back." (Luke 6:38 NLT)

This is called the Law of Reciprocity: what we share with others eventually comes back to us—somehow, some way, in some desirable form. It's one of life's great mysteries, but it works. And it applies not just to money, but also to love, acceptance, forgiveness...and time. There are many scriptures that reiterate this law, and unknowingly, even non-believers have embraced it, associating it with the idea of good karma and the phrase "what goes around comes around."

So, it actually pays to make time for others. Stop viewing people as interruptions to your plans. People aren't problems, but people often have problems. Help a few of them, and you help yourself. So, share your life. Share your resources: your money, your talents, your time! That's what you need to do if you really want to achieve your goals and, in the words of the Steve Miller Band, "fly like an eagle"!

Ask yourself, are you going to be a Time Lord or Time Hoard? What's a "Time Lord"? Doctor Who is a Time Lord. No, not doctor *who?* Doctor Who! —the eponymous hero of the BBC's long-running pop culture SF hit. The good Doctor travels through the past, present and future in his Tardis, a sentient time-defying spaceship, the exterior of which appears as an ordinary British police callbox. Doctor Who surfs through time looking for trouble. Hang on, that didn't exactly come out right. Doctor Who moves through time looking for problems he can fix and people he can help.

When you think about it, we're all moving through time, albeit in one direction, the future. And, like Doctor Who traveling in his Tardis, we may look like ordinary individuals passing the time, but we all have the potential to make a difference in our world. So, *who* are you: a Time Lord or a Time Hoard?

You Got to Be Ready, Jack!

Time and tide wait for no one.
—St. Marher, 1225

Imagine: It's Saturday and a good friend will be arriving at 6 p.m. to pick you up for a concert. You've wanted to hear this band play for a long time, and now's your big chance! While you're waiting for the doorbell to ring, you lie on the sofa in your pajamas and watch a few hours of reality TV. Your friend knocks at the door. You answer it. He takes one look at you and shakes his head in disbelief, because YOU'RE NOT READY! He's on a tight schedule, so he leaves without you. You just missed a golden opportunity. It's gone. Kaput. Finito. Sayonara.

What were you thinking? Were you even thinking? You shrug, slump back on the couch, and continue to watch the telly. Meanwhile, you're kicking yourself for not being ready, an oversight that has cost you an opportunity to fulfill your dream of hearing that new band.

Every big dream or goal works pretty much like the scenario we just imagined. When an opportunity comes along to move a step closer to fulfilling your own dreams, you need to be ready. When David Gerrold was growing up he knew he wanted to be a science fiction writer. In his book, *The Trouble with Tribbles*, he explains in the first chapter, "Getting Ready for Opportunity's Knock," how he got a chance to write a script for a major television SF drama. It was Gerrold's FIRST script ever and, once filmed and telecast, it proved to be one of the most popular episodes of the original *Star Trek*. Gerrold had made writing a successful script look easy, but he explains that it didn't just happen:

> "...I spent a lifetime training to be a *Star Trek* writer—even before I knew there was going to be a *Star Trek*... But even if it hadn't been *Star Trek*, it would have been something (else). That was the direction I was moving in. And *Star Trek* was the opportunity...."

Gerrold also points out that "...I was ready for the opportunity when it *did* occur. The G*O*L*D*E*N* O*P*P*O*R*T*U*N*I*T*Y* isn't worth a damn thing unless you're prepared to meet it. ...Once you make a decision to do something or to be something, start preparing for it immediately."

Like Gerrold, we may not know when or where our big break might come, but while we're waiting for it, we need to be learning, studying, training, practicing, and watching for it; taking the right steps, or at least trying to take steps, down the path to reach our goals. Don't wait till someone's ringing the doorbell to put your pants on. By then, it may be too late to get dressed. The delivery man has a schedule to keep, and he'll probably leave long before you can get to the door. If this happens to you, let's just hope he leaves your "dream delivery" on the front step.

"I know all the things you do, and I have opened a door for you that no one can close." (Revelation 3:8 NLT)

IN THE COILS OF THE CREATOR

President George W. Bush declared it the national toy of the United States; and in his 2002 State of the Union address he stated, "I cannot think of a recreational device that better exemplifies the inventiveness of the American spirit."

Over the last 70 years it's sold well over 300 million units.

It owes its unique ability to descend a staircase to "simple harmonic motion," the mechanics of which are governed by Hooke's Law and gravity. (*Huh?!?* Don't worry about this particular point; we promise there won't be a quiz.)

In 1995, it got a plum role in Pixar's *Toy Story*. What on earth are we discussing? According to the popular jingle sung on numerous TV commercials, "a spring, a spring—a marvelous *thing!* Everyone knows it's Slinky." —And it was created by accident!

In 1943, at a shipyard in Philadelphia, a naval mechanical engineer named Richard James was designing support springs that would be able to cushion and stabilize sensitive shipboard instruments during rough seas. He accidentally knocked one of his springs from a shelf, and was amazed to see it "step" down a stack of books, then walk across his worktable, before finally doing a summersault onto the floor. James the inventor instantly recognized a good thing, and he was ready to run with it. When he got home that evening, he told his wife, Betty, that he wanted to experiment further with the spring. He was convinced that—using the right properties of steel, and finding the perfect tension—he could create a toy that walked all by itself. James' wife was skeptical, until—after a year of fiddling with various springs—HE DID IT!

James unveiled his creation to a group of neighborhood kids who all cheered the "sleek and graceful" new toy. Wife Betty decided to call it a Slinky, which means...um..."sleek and graceful." Okay, trivia time: the original Slinky was two and a half inches tall and was made of 98 coils of high-grade blue-black Swedish steel. A local machine shop produced the first batch of 400 units; and initially, Richard and Betty James had trouble convincing toy stores to carry the product. The Gimbels department store in Philadelphia finally allowed the couple to set up an inclined plank in the toy section, where they demonstrated the Slinky to wide-eyed kids and their parents. Those first 400 units—each hand-wrapped in bright yellow paper and priced at $1—sold out in 90 minutes.

But that's nothing. During its first two years, the newly-formed James Industries sold 100 million Slinkys at a dollar apiece. Adjusting for inflation, that's equivalent to $1 Billion!

In 1960, Richard James left the company, and Betty took sole ownership; and she continued to preside over the ever-growing business until 1998. During those 38 years, she insisted on keeping the price of the original Slinky affordable. Betty once told *The New York Times*, "So many children can't have expensive toys, and I feel a real obligation to them."

And what of Richard? After creating one of the most unique and unusual, most popular and profitable, toys ever known, what does a millionaire inventor do for an encore? Well, after leaving his company in 1960, Richard James became an evangelical missionary in Bolivia with Wycliffe Bible Translators. Strange? That's not for us to decide.

But what's the lesson in the Story of Slinky? That's not for us to decide, either. There are several things we can take from this tale. For us to single out any one of them would minimize the others. What did *you* take from it?

Bon Appétit!

Innovative people have always had their fair share of critics: "It'll NEVER work!"; "It'll never FLY!"; "It'll never FLOAT!"; "It'll never stay SUBMERGED!" Anyone who knows their history, has learned to NEVER say "Never"! Still, many of us, as creators, are on the receiving end of the "No can do" attitudes and criticisms of certain agents, editors, publishers, financiers, and other assorted people who choose to see all the obstacles to any given project or goal. For your encouragement, we'll now share the story of a creator and her naysayers. And since we've been discussing cookbooks in our *Angel in the Kitchen* series, we've chosen as our subject, the late Julia Child, who wrote one of the most influential cookbooks of the 20th Century.

Julia Child was born in Pasadena, California, on August 15, 1912. Although she's internationally recognized as a multiple award-winning chef, author and television personality—as well as THE person who introduced and popularized French cooking in America—she attained none of this notoriety until she'd reached the ripe age of 51. Late bloomer? Some things are worth waiting for.

Many of us remember Julia Child as the elderly and unassuming French chef with the unusual voice that seemed to warble. It's interesting to learn that as a teenager, the six-foot, two-inch-tall Julia participated in sports while attending Smith College, and was an avid basketball player. She graduated from Smith in 1934 with a BA in English. Her career in cooking was still decades away. Long before she was "The French Chef," she moved to New York City and worked as a copywriter for the advertising department of a firm that marketed upscale home furnishings. She returned to California in 1937 and spent the next four years writing for local publications.

During World War II, Child tried to enlist, in both the WACs (Women's Army Corp) and the U.S. Navy's WAVES, but was rejected for being "too tall"! So, Child joined the famed OSS (Office of Strategic Services) and worked her way up from typist, to a top secret research position. While working in the Secret Intelligence division, Child had a variety of jobs that took her to Washington, D.C., Sri Lanka (Ceylon), and eventually to China. But her most interesting assignment may have been as the assistant to a research team developing shark repellent! The foul-tasting stuff was needed to keep sharks from exploding mines intended for German U-boats. So how in the world did Julia Child end up as the last word on French cuisine?

While in Ceylon, she met fellow OSS employee and New Jersey native Paul Cushing Child. The two were married in 1946, and moved to Paris, two years later, when Paul was given an assignment there by the US State Department. Julia's hubby was an artist, a poet, and a gourmet, and he introduced her to fine French cuisine—which she repeatedly described as a culinary revelation: "an opening up of the soul and spirit for me."

While in Paris, Julia attended the famous cooking school Le Cordon Bleu, and later studied with several master chefs. She also met Simone Beck and Louisette Bertholle, two French women who were trying to write a French cookbook for American readers. They quickly convinced Julia "the English major" to collaborate with them. That was around 1951, and the three cookbook creators spent the next decade researching and repeatedly testing recipes. Child translated the French into English, and worked to make the recipes detailed and interesting to American cooks. Finally, their book was finished. All they needed to do was find a New York publisher. Piece of cake?

The three authors were told repeatedly that their 726-page manuscript was "too long"! Other objections included: "No one's interested in preparing gourmet food"; "No one's buying cookbooks these days"; "If someone wants a recipe, they'll just tear it out of a magazine"! When a door finally opened, and Houghton-Mifflin signed them to a contract, the editors then rejected the manuscript because it seemed too much like an encyclopedia.

Alfred A. Knopf Company ultimately published *Mastering the Art of French Cooking* in 1961. It was a critically-acclaimed bestseller, and it's still in print to this day. More books followed, as well as a long-running television show. And would you believe, the kitchen set, where for years Julia Child cooked up special dishes for her legions of viewers, is now permanently exhibited in the Smithsonian.

So, all her naysayers had to eat crow—and at the end of each episode of *The French Chef*, Julia would say, "Bon appétit!"

"And the LORD answered me: 'Write the vision; make it plain.... For still the vision awaits its appointed time; ...If it seems slow, wait for it; it will surely come.'"

(Habakkuk 2:2-3 ESV)

Doughnuts, Dreams and Dedication!

Like beautiful clouds against a bright blue sky, our fondest, unfulfilled dreams often shift and subtly change shape—but never substance. Circumstances, time, and new insights all have a way of gently reshaping the "clouds" we chase. But the heart of those clouds, the basic ideas and areas of our greatest goals and dreams, usually remain intact.

When you have a good idea, stick with it—even through tough times. And if you do one single thing really well, and profitably, stay focused on that avocation, item, area. When you finally get something right, don't change it. Innovate all around it, finding new ways to use it, promote it, share it, market it—but why change the core vision as long as it's viable?

Some things, we're happy to say, don't change. These things were fine from the beginning, and they're still pretty wonderful. So why tamper with success? Vernon Rudolph understood this; since 1945, times have changed, but his delicious signature "Original Glazed Doughnut" has been a constant comfort food.

Vernon Carver Rudolph was born in Marshall County, Kentucky. In 1933, at age 18, Vernon began working for his uncle who owned a small general store in Paducah, Kentucky. That same year, Vernon's uncle, Ishmael, had purchased a secret recipe for yeast-raised doughnuts from a New Orleans chef who was working on an Ohio River barge, and was famous for his light and fluffy doughnuts. Although Ishmael's store sold a wide variety of goods, it was his delicious doughnuts that brought the customers in. A good thing, which helped the business to weather the Great Depression.

In the summer of 1937, Vernon started pursuing his dream: he was determined to own his own store, and specifically a doughnut shop. He moved to Winston-Salem, North Carolina and rented a building in what is now the historic Old Salem district. He started off by making and selling his doughnuts to local grocery stores.

Each night between the hours of midnight to around four in the morning, the streets were filled with the intoxicating aroma of fresh doughnuts baking. To say that Vernon's industry was disturbing the public peace would be an understatement. Neighbors started knocking on the door at obscene hours, asking if they could buy hot doughnuts. So, Vernon decided to cut a hole in a side wall of his shop, and started selling warm glazed doughnuts directly to customers on the sidewalk. But mind you, the warm doughnuts were only available during the wee hours of the night. We're not positive, but there's a good chance that Vernon not only created one of the first fast food service windows, but also got people addicted to the nightlife!

More innovations continued. In the early 1940s, Vernon started selling franchises. By 1944, he was selling a large variety of cake doughnuts in addition to the "Original Glazed Doughnut," and he decided to implement a devious new method to torment his clientele: he realized the unused space beneath the service counter could be put to better use; so he installed display cases showing off his frosted temptations.

In 1947, Vernon founded the Krispy Kreme Corporation, and trademarked the familiar green and red bowtie logo, which had been designed for him by a local architect. In 1955, Krispy Kreme started a fundraising program which allowed schools and churches to purchase and resell doughnuts, helping these organizations to buy books, uniforms and needed equipment.

In 1963, Krispy Kreme went from hand making doughnuts to automated production—but the recipe stayed the same, as well as the taste. Vernon Rudolph continued to innovate around his core idea, his original delicious doughnuts—unchanged through decades of marketing and expansion. Today, Krispy Kreme is known internationally, with stores in Canada, South America, the Dominican Republic, and almost 100 donut shops in Mexico alone. But wherever you go, Vernon's standard of excellence is enforced: "...Impeccable presentation is critical wherever Krispy Kreme is sold...."

Determination can be delicious, and presentation powerful. But never change a good thing. Market and innovate around it. Find your passion and stick with it!

"God wouldn't change His plan. He wanted to make this perfectly clear to those who would receive His promise...." (Hebrews 6:17 GOD'S WORD)

Another Nasty Naysayer who Knew Nothing!

During the mid-1960s, a college freshman signed up for a seminar in creative writing. She'd been recommended by the head of the English department, who apparently saw her potential.

After a few assignments, she was called into the office of the visiting Harvard professor instructing the seminar. He told the seventeen-year-old student, "...Your writing stinks." Not a very encouraging thing to say to someone who's trying to learn and develop a craft. Who knows, maybe what she'd turned in needed a lot of polish? On the other hand, it's possible the traveling professor may have simply taken a disliking to the girl, who'd indirectly mentioned she was Catholic.

The professor went on to tell the girl she had no business being in his class, or pursuing writing as a career. He said, "...You'll never earn a dime as a writer." He then convinced her to give up on her dream of being a novelist.

Catherine Lanigan, the impressionable young student, changed her major and gave up on writing. Fourteen years later, she had a chance meeting with a "Barnabas": a writer who took an interest in her stolen dream and agreed to read her unpublished novel—a ragged stack of pages she never had the heart to discard. The writer liked what he read and immediately forwarded Catherine's retyped pages to his own agent—who promptly signed the stunned young woman to a publishing contract.

Today, Catherine has published over three dozen books, including novels and collections of inspirational articles. She's earned far more than "a dime as a writer"! Her only lament is that she took the advice of a naysayer and wasted a lot of years, when she could have been writing, creating, and following her one true dream.

Don't ever allow anyone to steal your dream. There will always be naysayers among your friends and family members. People who will pontificate over you, your talents (or alleged lack thereof), and your future fortunes. Elvis, "the King of Rock and Roll," was told he'd never make it as a singer; Edison, "the Wizard of Menlo Park," that he'd never amount to anything; Stallone, the internationally known movie star, that he couldn't act; and the list goes on.

People, as we've previously discussed, can find a multitude of reasons for being critical: fear and jealousy, lack of faith, or simply a negative spirit. If you listen to the wrong people, if you take the wrong advice, you can stall in the pursuit of your dreams.

Remember, every single day some very "ordinary" people—just like you and us—become writers and artists, actors and filmmakers, singers and musicians, inventors and entrepreneurs. Not because anyone said they could be, and not necessarily because there was anything extraordinarily special about them—other than their determination not to give in. Successful people are hardheaded that way!

So, take the opinions of the naysayers with a grain of salt. Shake off the rejection. Get back to work. Follow your dream to create. "So encourage each other and build each other up...." (1 Thessalonians 5:11 NLT)

GOT AGGRAVATIONS?
NO SWEAT!

Smile and the world smiles back at you! Right? Well, not always. Our society has its fair share of scrooges and sourpusses, bigots and bad seeds.

We can't control how people will treat us in this life. We can't make them value us or our work. We have no control over whether they will value our abilities or even show us respect. And we should never try to force any of these things! We have better things to do than deal with the shortcomings of those bad eggs we daily encounter. For one, we should be far more concerned, and far busier, about the business of pursuing our dreams and achieving our goals.

We can't change people or their perceptions. But we CAN control how we'll respond to their treatment. We can let their stares and suspicious looks, their critical comments and nasty attitudes, penetrate and get under our skin—or we can let it all bounce off our backs as we face new horizons and explore promising opportunities. In other words, we don't need to spend any precious time or emotional energy on what others are saying. Ignore Negative Nancy, Bobby Badmouther,

Pessimistic Patty, Jealous Johnny, Debbie Downer, and Arguing Andy.

Nothing can steal your peace and zap your creativity faster than being around these "foul friends" and engaging in their toxic emotions. We can "entertain" thoughts of frustration, anger, unforgiveness, and rejection—and allow such strong emotions to poison us and our prospects; or we can choose to "flip the channel" and get on with more important stuff. Big stuff, not "small stuff"!

In his book, *Don't Sweat the Small Stuff*, Dr. Richard Carlson, Ph.D. states: "The first step in becoming a more peaceful person is to have the humility to admit that, in most cases, you're creating your own emergencies. Life will usually go on if things don't go according to plan." Beyond our social interactions, a few of the other things that often tend NOT to go as we planned are our schedules, the weather, the price of gas, the traffic conditions, even the lines at the grocery store. We can't change these things, so we need to have a victorious attitude concerning them.

Dr. Carlson suggests several tips for a victorious attitude. For instance:

"Life is not an emergency"! We don't need the added pressure of feeling we must achieve a certain number of things each day. This perception keeps us in a frenzy. So chill! Tomorrow's another day.

"Refuse to let it bug you": no matter what someone else says or believes, when you get down to it, it's JUST their opinion. Should you allow their erroneous, misinformed, or biased opinions to get in your way? Of course not! Besides, you *should* be too focused on achieving your dreams to notice their silly comments.

"See the innocence"! People are flawed, just like us. They've experienced their own hurts and disappointments, and these feelings often come out in their words

138

and actions. Understanding this is another big step toward not being offended.

"Think of your problems as potential teachers"; we can learn something from every "kooky character" we meet, every "sorry circumstance" we find ourselves in. If we allow God to work in us, He will grow *peace, patience, love and forgiveness* from the "dirt" of our adversity.

But the best tip we can give you comes from God's Word: "You will keep in perfect peace all who trust in you, all whose thoughts are fixed on you!" (Isaiah 26:3 NLT)

Dwell on God's faithfulness and *His* goodness, not on *your* problems and *other* people. Don't waste your emotional (and creative) energy fretting over "fouls"; or attempting to fix your friends (or "enemies")! Concentrate on God's destiny for your life. Don't sweat the small stuff—and, as Dr. Carlson states, "...It's all small stuff."

THE WORST THAT COULD HAPPEN....

A while back, during the television show *Hour of Power*, host Bobby Schuller asked his guest, an entrepreneur, to share a few details about his journey to success. The young man related how he'd mailed out 250 letters asking different people who'd made it big, if they could help him to realize his own dream. Out of those 250 requests, he received only a single response! Not very encouraging; but nevertheless the enterprising young man should be applauded for doing something few of us seem to have the courage to do these days: he needed help, so he asked for a helping hand.

Somehow, during the journey from childhood to mature adult, most people lose the confidence or the boldness or the freedom to ask *anyone* for *anything*. Adults actually hate asking. Most assume the answer will be a "no" anyway, so why waste the time. At work, there's even an old expression, "It's easier to ask for forgiveness than for permission"!

Nobody likes to face rejection, and a "NO" leaves us out in the cold, standing there with our hat in our hand, looking stupid—*or so we think*. At worst, a *no* is simply a *no*, and it often just means "not now" or "not here"; but at best, a *no* is nothing more than one of the tiniest words in the English language that means "keep on knocking, keep on trying"! And yet, adults fear the word. In fact, the thought of getting a NO! paralyzes them to the point where they'd rather be drawn and quartered than ask for something—especially help.

Pride may also play into their stubbornness, as well as the idea they might be inconveniencing someone. If only we could recapture the freedom and fearlessness of childhood. Kids don't worry about silly stuff, and they don't hesitate to ask for *anything*. If a child's friend has only one cookie, most assuredly the child will ask if he can have half of it. An ice cream cone? "Can I have a lick or two?" True, most kids have no sense of propriety, but they also aren't limited by the foolish fear of a "NO"!

Sons and daughters know it never hurts to ask mom and dad for a new bike or, a few years later, if they can borrow the car. Why should they? The worst that could happen is they hear the tiny word *no*. But to a child the sky's the limit: the answer just might be a glorious, filled-with-possibilities YES!! God wants us to have that same childlike faith. He wants us to view life as filled with possibilities. God also wants us to ask Him for the things we need and even some of the things we simply want. After all, He's our Heavenly Father, and it never hurts to ask. Sometimes His answer will be "NO"; but when it *is* a *no*, God certainly has His reasons—and they're always good reasons.

Nevertheless, God expects us to be confident and make our requests known to Him. "Do not be anxious about anything, but in every situation, by prayer and petition, with thanksgiving, present your requests to God." (Philippians 4:6 NLT) Now, if we can ask the God of the Universe, then why can't we ask each other for help?

We've asked store managers to honor their sales beyond the deadline—and received a *YES*. One of us once asked to be considered for a job that required far more experience—and got both a YES and the job! Hey, nothing ventured, nothing gained! So ASK already! Want a raise, or time off? Want a date with someone you think is special? Want to marry that special person? Want a loan? Want a customer to buy your new product or service? Want a publisher to buy your book?

Want the kids to help out at home? Want your spouse to change a bad habit? *Have you asked?* Again, the worst that can happen is you hear a NO. But imagine a YES, instead. Remember: "You do not have because you do not ask." (James 4:2 NASB)

Do you need a "Barnabas" to help you reach a goal or fulfill a dream? Then open your mouth and ask! You just might make the connection you need to get to the next level. That's the power of asking! Remember that young entrepreneur we mentioned? The one who asked 250 people for help. He didn't even get the courtesy of a response from 249 of them. But none of that mattered, because the single response he *did* get was a "yes" from Donald Trump! So yes, it definitely pays to ask.

Don't Make Yourself Too Comfortable!

Thomas Edison once stated, "Discontent is the first necessity of progress." If you examine many of the innovations of the 20th Century, and ponder the motivations behind them, you'll understand Edison was right. No one invents anything simply to prove it can be done. Innovators (and dreamers) aren't like mountain climbers; they don't accomplish something great "because it's there!"

Vaccines are developed when disease threatens our civilization; faster modes of transportation because people are...well, in a hurry; smaller, smarter, more powerful phones and tablets because we want to be able to communicate, access information, and enjoy all the other benefits of computers on the go and with less to lug around. The point is, when a society finds itself in an undesirable situation, or isn't satisfied with its level of comfort or convenience, it generally responds with the innovations necessary to elevate itself from its troubling circumstances.

What was the motivation behind the invention of the electric light? Several people were striving to make it work—Edison stuck with it until he succeeded—but why so much interest? Well, can you imagine what it was like to read by a kerosene lamp? Or worse, a flickering candle? Edison and others weren't satisfied with these relatively poor sources of light. They wanted something better.

Many inventors such as Edison or Henry Ford also wanted to solve a specific problem. Ford used the assembly line to overcome time constraints in production. Milton S. Hershey formulated a chocolate bar that resisted melting at temperatures above 90 degrees Fahrenheit because U.S. troops in WWII needed just such a bar.

Edison goes on to state, "Show me a thoroughly satisfied man and I'll show you a failure." A strong statement—which may sound illogical as well as unbiblical. It's neither. When we're comfortable, we're not challenged to change and, specifically, to improve. If we're satisfied with where we are in life, we'll stop trying to go higher. Getting back to Edison's first statement, when we're discontent with our surroundings, our wasteful or harmful habits, our spiritual state, we're more likely to make the necessary changes. Discontent is a powerful motivator. Which is why, in life, many people have to hit rock bottom before they get fed up enough to finally change.

So, in life, in innovation, in our relationships with God and the people around us, we never want to become complacent. Now, this doesn't mean we should become discontent with what the Lord has blessed us with. The Apostle Paul said, "I know what it is to be in need, and I know what it is to have plenty. I have learned the secret of being content in any and every situation, whether well fed or hungry, whether living in plenty or in want. I can do all this through him who gives me strength." (Philippians 4:12-13 NIV) To do anything less is to present our Lord with an ungrateful spirit. On the other hand, we should always strive to improve ourselves, our circumstances, and the circumstances and conditions of others. Let us all work together to make the world a better place.

If you're pursuing a dream or trying to achieve a goal, you're more likely to achieve it once you make up your mind NOT to be complacent. Make the most of whatever situation you're in, and by all means, be happy! But don't get too comfortable. Aim higher. And then, when you find yourself overworked and underpaid, unchallenged and confined, by a job, a relationship, etc., you'll probably also discover the motivation you need to pay the price, to do what it takes to succeed, or to change.

People who are comfortable tend to stay right where they are, whether it's the recliner in front of the TV or a job that's "not great but pays pretty good." So, don't get comfortable—unless you're planning on staying for a while. Be discontent enough to climb out, climb higher, keep on climbing. Not because "it's *there*" but because you long for something better, greater, nobler.

"Jabez prayed to the God of Israel: Please bless me and give me more territory. May your power be with me and free me from evil so that I will not be in pain. God gave him what he prayed for." (1 Chronicles 4:10 GOD'S WORD)

A Duo of Diversified

Dentists!

It never hurts to diversify. After all, why put all your eggs (or gifts and talents) into one basket? And if you're a creator, that means devoting time and energy to both your day job *and* your creative hobbies and sidelines. Even when that hobby doesn't seem to fit in with your "chosen" profession. Take William James Morrison (1860-1926) for instance. He was a dentist by trade. It's hard to imagine he'd do anything that didn't fit in with his day job. But you'd be surprised.

Morrison apparently wanted more out of life than filling cavities. He was an avid inventor, and owing to his creative nature, the good dentist held a number of patents in his name—for gadgets and gizmos you'd never expect from someone whose jurisdiction is teeth. Enough suspense. Morrison invented the first cotton candy machine! (But, now that we think about it, maybe Morrison was trying to grow his dental practice.)

The New York Times once wrote that cotton candy "is almost 99.999 percent sugar, with dashes of flavoring and food coloring." Good for the teeth! Whether Morrison was enjoying the irony of his connection to the sweet stuff, or simply trying to disguise what he was selling, isn't known; but the dentist named his puffy confection "fairy floss"! We get it, though: floss with these sugary strands and the tooth fairy will be frequently visiting your pillow.

Today, cotton candy is still called fairy floss in Australia and South Africa. In the UK, Ireland, New Zealand and India, it's called candy floss. In Canada, as well as here in the U.S., we use the more descriptive COTTON candy. But a rose by any other name is...well, still just a form of spun sugar.

Cotton candy is mostly made of air. A typical serving size weighs about an ounce (30 grams). The confection is created by heating, and thus liquifying sugar; and then rapidly spinning a cylinder containing the liquid sugar, forcing the syrup out through tiny holes. The extruded sugar then re-solidifies in wispy strands of "sugar glass."

Prior to Morrison's 1897 invention of the electric "fairy floss" machine, making spun sugar was an expensive and labor-intensive endeavor. Hence, spun sugar was not widely available. Nor was it affordable to the average person. Today, cotton candy is a traditional and relatively inexpensive treat sold at carnivals, circuses, and fairs—with the airy confection either wound about a paper cone or stuffed into a plastic bag. Morrison introduced his machine at the 1904 St. Louis World's Fair, and his fairy floss was an instant hit. The dentist sold over 68,000 boxes at 25¢ per box, which today is equivalent to $6 per box.

We mentioned earlier the importance of diversification. Morrison was also a lawyer, an author, and a civic leader. Oh yeah, and later he became the President of the Tennessee State Dental Association.

Several years later, in 1921, Joseph Lascaux, yet another dentist, from New Orleans, Louisiana, invented a similar fairy floss machine. This "tooth doctor" gets the credit for coming up with the more straightforward name "cotton candy," which he quickly patented. What was it with dentists and sugar? Just part of our wonderfully whacky world, we guess. And the ultimate statement in diversification.

Now go thou and diversify—and remember: "Whatever you do, do it enthusiastically, as something done for the Lord and not for men...."

(Colossians 3:23 Holman Christian Standard Bible)

Just Do the Work!

My tongue is the pen of a speedy writer.
—Psalm 45:1 Young's Literal Translation

What do the Lone Ranger, the Green Hornet, and Sergeant Preston of the Yukon have in common? All three characters debuted in popular weekly radio shows, and all three were created (at the behest of George W. Trendle, who owned Detroit radio station WXYZ) by a college dropout!

What would you do if your boss asks you to create a radio adventure show set in the American Wild West and featuring a masked hero similar to Zorro—only different? *Oh yeah*, and give the masked man an ethnic sidekick. After your new show becomes a hit, he tells you to create another show exactly like it, featuring a similar masked character...with an ethnic sidekick—except you should make it different. What if your boss then demands you create a third adventure show, this time starring a dog, but not like Lassie? Your boss wants a rough and tumble working dog, not a pet.

If you're Fran Striker, and your boss is signing your weekly paycheck, you simply nod, put on your thinking cap, start typing, and...*well*, you JUST DO IT! No excuses, no mulling it over, and no writer's block allowed. After centuries of storytelling, the truth is, there are no original plots or new characters left in fiction, only variations of variations. Striker understood this. He knew that all that was left was to tell a good story, get it in on time, and then quickly start another. You just do the work. Does this sound like the attitude of a hack writer? We guess it all depends on how much work the writer invests into each new story, how effective the storytelling is, how successful the work turns out.

Fran Striker scripted 156 episodes of *The Lone Ranger* a year—for close to twenty years—in addition to writing 12 novels and hundreds of scripts for many other radio shows. He wrote for 14 hours a day, producing 60,000 words of fiction each day, and he wore out 4 typewriters in the process! Striker worked hard and conscientiously, his stories were immensely entertaining and popular, and his radio characters have become iconic, making the transition to other media including TV, movies and comic books. A hack? Not in the least. Besides, there are far easier ways to make a living.

American writer Fran Striker was born in Buffalo, New York, on August 19, 1903. He quit college to get into local theatre. A year later he got a job as a radio announcer, and eventually became station manager. Partly from opportunity, but mostly out of necessity, he started writing for the medium. Writing for radio in the 1930s was a demanding occupation, but Striker had a

DIET FOR DREAMERS

formula that guaranteed he'd never run out of stories. Want to know it?

Striker composed several lists: all the various personality types; a list of problems, challenges and obstacles to life (physical, financial, social, occupational, etc.); as well as a list of character strengths; and an extremely long list of character flaws and weaknesses. Striker would pick one or two items from each of his lists, tie them together and then write the resultant story. His methodology never failed him. And because mixing and matching items from his lists provided him with hundreds of plot variations, his creative well never ran dry. Striker knew all he had to do was pound the typewriter keys—to just do the work. And he did.

"It has all been done before. Nothing under the sun is truly new." (Ecclesiastes 1:9 NLT)

MONKEES MOM MAKES MONEY MANUFACTURING!

She was a young working mom, and she came up with a great idea; an idea so good, yet so obvious, she was surprised no one had already thought of it. An invention that was the perfect solution to an aggravating problem. And she formulated her invention in her own kitchen.

Bette Nesmith Graham was born in Dallas, Texas in 1924, and raised in San Antonio. After her father passed away in the early 1950s, Bette moved back to Dallas with her son, Michael (who was destined to become a member of the legendary rock band The Monkees), and her sister. The three took up residence there, in a house Bette's father had left to her; and Bette quickly got a job as a secretary for a Texas bank, in order to help support her family.

Bette eventually worked her way up to the position of executive secretary. She also worked weekends painting holiday display windows for the bank. She once said of her painting sideline, "[when] lettering, an artist never corrects by erasing, but always paints over the error."

Bette couldn't use the same technique on her day job, which demanded a lot of typing. Whenever she made a mistake, it had to be laboriously erased. But erasing mistakes was becoming more difficult. The bank switched to electric typewriters, and any rubber eraser stubble that found its way into the mechanical workings would gum up the typewriter. Bette's solution was to correct her mistakes the same way she did when painting window displays.

"...I decided to use what artists use. I put some tempera water-based paint in a bottle and took my watercolor brush to the office. I used that to correct my mistakes." The bank didn't approve of this radical method of "whiting out" typos, but Graham continued to secretly use her correction paint for five years. During this time, her corrections largely went unnoticed by her bank bosses—proof that her invention worked.

Bette continued to improve her formula, and her coworkers frequently asked to borrow her "paint out." In 1956, she decided to market her typewriter correction fluid as "Mistake Out."

Shortly after Bette founded the Mistake Out Company, she had a bit of bad luck: the bank fired her from her typist job. While typing a letter, she inadvertently inserted the name of her own company, instead of the bank's! Had she caught her mistake, she could have simply painted it out! But misfortune can often work on our behalf: now jobless, Bette decided to devote all her time to her new business.

During the 1960s Bette manufactured, bottled, and sold Mistake Out in her home—mixing the white fluid in her kitchen blender! As her correction fluid caught on and soon became an indispensable tool of the secretarial trade, she relocated production and shipping to a 10x26-foot shed in her backyard.

When business seemed more than she could handle, she offered to sell her formula to IBM. The corporation wasn't interested. So Bette continued to sell her correction fluid from her home for another 17 years.

She eventually changed the product name to *Liquid Paper*, and at the height of her business, she employed 200 people who manufactured 25 million bottles of correction fluid a year.

In 1979 Bette sold the Liquid Paper Company to the Gillette Corporation for $47.5 million. Not bad for a simple idea that started as a cottage industry.

"We know that all things work together for the good of those who love God—those whom he has called according to his plan." (Romans 8:28 GOD'S WORD)

Do It Yourself Success!

Can art be orchestrated? Can success be engineered? Apparently the answer is a resounding YES! Especially when you recruit all the right people to help. That's exactly what Bob Rafelson did in the 1960s. Although it was never what the aspiring filmmaker intended.

Rafelson developed an unusual concept for a TV series in 1962: the weekly misadventures of a rising rock and roll band. Rafelson had his eye on singer-songwriter John Sebastion and his Greenwich Village folk-rock group The Lovin' Spoonful. Sebastion's quartet would eventually top the charts with such hits as "Summer in the City" and "Do You Believe in Magic"; but at the time the four musicians were relatively unknown and looking for precisely the exposure Rafelson's new series could afford them.

Rafelson pitched his idea to Universal Studio's television section and received the first of several rejections. So he shelved the project and went to work for Screen Gems, where he met his soon-to-be collaborator Bert Schneider. In 1965, after the phenomenal success of The Beatles' movie, *A Hard Day's Night*—about the misadventures of a rising rock and roll band—Rafelson realized that the television money men might now be open to his series concept. He and Schneider repackaged the idea and easily sold it to Screen Gems.

Unfortunately, during the time it took to sell the show, a new wrinkle had developed: The Lovin' Spoonful finally got its big break, when the four musicians were signed to a lucrative and very exclusive record contract. No problem, though. When a wide door of opportunity suddenly shuts, just find yourself an open window to crawl through! Rafelson and Schneider decided they'd simply create their own pop group. After all, it shouldn't be that hard to locate and assemble four young, attractive and talented guys who were also totally cool and musically inclined.

Rafelson already had his eye on British actor Davy Jones, who'd recently been nominated for a Tony Award for his supporting role in the Broadway musical *Oliver!* Jones could both sing and act, and he had teen-idol good looks to boot. Then came Micky Dolenz, a former child actor who'd starred in the TV show *Circus Boy* and then later played guitar for a dubious group called The Missing Links. Third and fourth up were Michael Nesmith and Peter Tork.

Peter Tork played a fair guitar and had been working in various Greenwich Village clubs. He heard about the casting call from his pal Stephen Stills, who'd auditioned for a part but had been rejected. And yes, if you know your music history, you probably realize this is THE Stephen Stills of the legendary group Crosby, Stills and Nash—one of the greatest guitarists of all time.

Michael Nesmith, who'd been seriously and actively pursuing a musical career, actually answered the ad he chanced upon in the *Daily Variety*, casting for "4 insane boys, age 17-21." Nesmith got a part, and Rafelson got exactly what he advertised for: a quartet of four insane boys! Whenever the group was assembled in the recording studio, the youths would cut up and accomplish very little. In order to meet his schedule, Don Kirshner, who was orchestrating the "manufacturing" of the group's music, had to bring in the "band" members one at a time, and lay down each of their tracks individually.

Kirshner also brought in solid backup musicians, as well as professional songwriters such as Neil Diamond—because initially Rafelson's engineered rock band was far from being ready for prime time. But eventually the "4 insane boys" did get up to speed, enough to actually go on a successful music tour throughout North America and Europe...and The Monkees were born!

You knew we were discussing The Monkees, didn't you? Rafelson's made-for-TV rock band has sold more than 75 million records worldwide and had several international hits. At the height of their popularity in 1967, The Monkees outsold the Beatles and The Rolling Stones put together. Which definitely proves, if you have a dream, bring in the right people and work hard, you CAN make it happen!

Today, God is proclaiming that He is faithful; He is the promise-keeper; He is the fulfiller of dreams. He has not forsaken you. He knows all your greatest hopes and aspirations. Trust in Him, and hold on to your dreams! "Delight yourself in the LORD, and He will give you the desires of your heart." (Psalm 37:4 ESV)

"...I am doing a new thing! Do you not perceive it? I am making a way in the wilderness...." (Isaiah 43:19 NIV)

You can join Tom & Wilma English each weekday for humorous and inspiring new articles at their website,

AngelAtTheDoor.com

www.ingramcontent.com/pod-product-compliance
Lightning Source LLC
Chambersburg PA
CBHW031318040426
42443CB00005B/130